The Duleep Singhs

THE PHOTOGRAPH ALBUM OF QUEEN VICTORIA'S MAHARAJAH

This book is dedicated to those great Sikh martyrs, who did not flinch once at the sight of death during the Sikh holocausts of 1746, 1762 and 1984, so that we may enjoy the fruits of freedom.

Waheguru ji ka Khalsa,
Waheguru ji ke fateh.

(The Pure belong to the Almighty,
Victory belongs to the Almighty)

The Duleep Singhs

THE PHOTOGRAPH ALBUM OF QUEEN VICTORIA'S MAHARAJAH

PETER BANCE

FOREWORD BY
CHRISTY CAMPBELL

SUTTON PUBLISHING

This book was first published in 2004 by
Sutton Publishing Limited · Phoenix Mill
Thrupp · Stroud · Gloucestershire · GL5 2BU

British Library Cataloguing in Publication Data
A catalogue record for this book is available from the British Library.

ISBN 0 7509 3488 3

Typeset in 13/18pt Bembo.
Typesetting and origination by
Sutton Publishing Limited.
Printed in Great Britain by
J.H. Haynes & Co. Ltd, Sparkford, England.

Contents

	Foreword by Christy Campbell	7
	Preface	9
	Introduction	11
1	The Birth of Duleep Singh	17
2	Life in England	27
3	Return to India & Marriage	35
4	The Suffolk Squire	45
5	To Europe	65
6	Princes Victor and Albert Edward	75
7	Prince Frederick	85
8	Princess Catherine	105
9	Princess Sophia	113
10	Princess Bamba	127
11	The Legacy of Maharajah Duleep Singh	135
	Family Tree	148
	Glossary	150
	References	151
	Bibliography	156
	Acknowledgements and Picture Credits	157
	Index	159

The tomb of Sardar Mahan Singh marks the place where Maharajah Duleep Singh's grandfather, Mahan Singh, was cremated in 1790, at Gujranwala in the Punjab. After the Independence of India and its subsequent partition in 1947, Gujranwala came under Pakistani rule and the shrine has since fallen into neglect.

Foreword

Maharajah Duleep Singh and photography came into the world together. In the autumn of 1838, while the court of Lahore rejoiced at the birth of Maharajah Ranjit Singh's son, in faraway France the scientist Louis Daguerre was perfecting a way of capturing natural light on a silver-coated copper plate. A portrait subject would have to stay stock-still for three minutes or more – but it worked. The past would no longer be a foreign country. Through the intervention of pioneer photographers, future generations could peer back into the faces of their ancestors, who, long ago, had themselves stared into a camera's lens.

I first discovered the story of the Maharajah through the printed word – letters, diaries and official documents. In my mind, however, a slideshow of images was constantly playing – the gorgeous display of Ranjit's court, the martial dramas of the Anglo-Sikh wars, and of the boy king Duleep, deposed from his throne and brought to London in all his finery as an exotic talisman for Queen Victoria.

There were more sombre mental images, too, of the middle-aged Duleep dressed in dark frockcoat or the rufous tweeds of the grouse-moor, of plotting top-hatted politicians and colonial administrators who sought to control his fate, of the Queen Empress corresponding with her wayward favourite from the gloom of Balmoral, the court still drenched in formal mourning.

Then, when I was investigating the politics of the Maharajah's story, I was lucky enough to meet Peter Bance, who kindly shared with me his years of pictorial research. Did I know there was a photograph of Duleep taken in India, when he was ten? In a London archive I held the frail original scrap (a 'calotype'), taken by an East India Company surgeon – one of the very first photographs made outside Europe. I was astonished.

But Peter had discovered so much more. Perhaps it was the early influence of Prince Albert (a keen amateur photographer), but, for whatever reason, a camera lens was never far from the exiled Maharajah and his family. As he fitfully pursued the life of a Norfolk country squire, the Maharajah's albums filled with images formal and informal – of his first wife Bamba, of royal hunting parties, of his young daughters tending their ponies on the lawns at Elveden, of his sons growing to maturity, half English gents in their velvet brocade jackets, half Sikh princes with their long hair.

That perhaps was Duleep's own dilemma. Was he the anglicized Christian gentleman his mentors so earnestly wished him to be, or the Sikh warrior whose destiny was to regain his stolen kingdom? He abandoned his family and slipped into the shadows, watched no longer by fashionable society but by the spies of HM Foreign Secret Service.

This amazing book captures an amazing life. The author continues the story of the Maharajah's family long after Duleep's own death, revealing the fates of his sons and daughters with brilliant new research. Peter Bance has brought a lost world back into the light.

Christy Campbell, 2004

Preface

From an early age I can remember being told about the past glories of the Sikh Kingdom, and the legendary Maharajah Ranjit Singh. I had heard about his infant son, who had inherited a kingdom larger than Great Britain, and how the kingdom had withered away, as had his existence. However, it was not until a quiet Sunday afternoon some seven years ago while driving through the Suffolk countryside with a friend that my interest in Maharajah Duleep Singh blossomed. We had heard of the Maharajah having been buried in Suffolk – but that was all we had to go on. Stumbling upon the graves of Duleep Singh and his family in a churchyard in Elveden we were told by a villager of a little museum in the nearby town of Thetford. Ten minutes later we were standing inside what could only be described as a shrine to this Sikh royal family. I discovered that I knew very little about the Maharajah, let alone his eight children, one of whom had given the town this very museum. I came home proud of what I had discovered, like an archaeologist with his new find, but at the same time disappointed with myself at not knowing about such an important part of my Sikh heritage, especially as this was on my doorstep, and not thousands of miles away in the Punjab.

My reading journey began; there was much to read, both by contemporary and modern writers. Cunningham's fine book on the Sikhs in 1849 was a masterpiece, while Emily Eden's experiences of meeting Ranjit Singh in 1838 provided a humorous and personal account. Maharajah Duleep Singh's two official biographies of 1882 and 1884 were scandalous and charming respectively. Modern writers have summed up much of what had been previously written, but there was no account of Duleep Singh's family, his two wives or his children. It was as if they had been phased out from history, their only record being in dusty photograph albums or in the memories of the elderly village folk.

Maharajah Duleep Singh's life can best be summed up by one word: 'tragic'. Born into one of the richest ruling houses in the world, he died a pauper forgotten not only by his peers but also by his own countrymen. As an innocent minor, Maharajah Duleep Singh enjoyed the plush life of a royal heir, but his untimely dethronement brought great turmoil. His arrival on the shores of England drew him into a different spotlight, and he captured the hearts of others to such an extent that the Empress of India herself accepted the Maharajah's colourful character and peculiar native habits with open arms. Her Majesty Queen Victoria showered affection upon the turbaned Maharajah, as did the Prince Consort. This most unlikely of alliances saw the start of a relationship of love and loyalty. The Maharajah was looked upon as an adopted son of Her Majesty, encouraged to mingle with the household, play with the younger princes and holiday with them at Osborne House. His dignified appearance and native ways were a sheer joy for the royal family, and this is evident in the delightful photograph taken by Prince Albert of his children, where little Prince Alfred, later the Grand Duke of Saxe-Coburg Gotha, and Prince Arthur, later the Duke of Connaught, appear in the Maharajah's turbans and Indian dress. Even Her Majesty practised her artistic skills by drawing sketches and watercolours of the handsome Sikh king in her sketchpad. The Maharajah's fondness for the weak Prince Leopold was touching, while his friendship with the Prince of Wales remained until the end. The devoted queen and Prince Consort became godparents to the Maharajah's eldest son Prince Victor, whom the Maharajah named after his most gracious sovereign. Invited to almost every royal gathering and wedding of his day, the Maharajah's presence added zest to every occasion. The big-spending Maharajah displayed all the characteristics of a Victorian prince: besides being a serial playboy, he was an avid shooting squire who also knew how to throw a party. But his fondness for the high life contributed to his demise as much as the injustice of the British establishment, whose inability to keep promises drove the Maharajah to foreign meddlers – although his allegiance to other European superpowers proved less than fruitful. His denouncement of his British way of life came back to haunt him, and he was forced to plead for forgiveness and pardon from his very first royal confidante, Her Majesty Queen Victoria.

The Maharajah may have died over a hundred years ago, but his legacy lives on. His name is always the first to be mentioned in tales of the British Raj, among them the ownership squabbles over the infamous Koh-i-noor diamond, that symbol of power, authority and wealth, once owned by the Maharajah, but which now sits resplendently on the late Queen Mother's state crown. Then there are the stories surrounding the mysterious end to the Maharajah's lineal descendants, as none of his eight children had any issue. This possibly arises from the curse of a Guru's prophecy, or Queen Victoria's part in making the royal family of Lahore extinct for the security of her empire.

Introduction

The earliest known ancestor of Maharajah Duleep Singh was a Sansi Jat farmer called Desu. Born in 1670,[1] he owned about 25 acres of land near Gujranwala, known as 'Sukarchak'. After being baptised as a Sikh, he was renamed Budh Singh and joined fellow Sikhs in the fight against injustice and religious persecution at the hands of the Mughal authorities.

Budh Singh died in 1716 of apoplexy, leaving two sons, Naudh Singh and Chanda Singh, the latter settling in Raja Sansi and adopting the name of Sandhawalia. India's ruling Mughal dynasty at Delhi had crumbled, and the Punjab had become prey to looting and plundering from the Middle East. The Sikhs formed confederacies known as Misals,[2] each of which ruled their own areas of the Punjab by receiving a Rakhi system from villagers.[3] Naudh Singh formed his own Misal in 1748, which became known as the Sukarchakkia Misal. It was one of the twelve Misals formed to fight against oppression, foreign invaders and plunderers. Although each Misal ruled its own territory, it would join forces with others in the event of an outside attack.

In 1749 Naudh Singh was wounded in the head by a gun shot while fighting the Afghans. The wound did not prove fatal but he was incapacitated, and lingered on for a few years without any active participation in the Sikh movement in the Punjab. He died in 1752. His wife, Lali, had borne him four sons, the most prominent being Charhat Singh. In a short period of fifteen years, Charhat Singh became the master of the regions of Gujranwala, Wazirabad, Sialkot, Pind Dadun Khan and Rohtas. However, the success was short lived: his own matchlock exploded during fighting against the Afghan army of Ahmed Shah Abdali in 1774. On Charhat Singh's death, his young son Mahan Singh was brought into the arena, and proved to be an inspirational leader. He further increased the Misal's territory, and married the daughter of the Raja of Jind.[4] Mahan Singh showed great political qualities by marrying his only son Ranjit Singh to Mehtab Kaur in 1786. Mehtab Kaur was the only child of another great Misal leader, a widow by the name of Sardarni Sada Kaur, the head of the powerful Kanaiya Misal. The

Kanaiya Misal at the time were enemies of the Sukarchakkias, as it was common belief that the Sukarchakkias had a hand in the killing of Sada Kaur's husband. But this clever matrimonial coup by Mahan Singh was a stroke of genius, bringing both families and Misals together into one powerful fighting force.

Mahan Singh's death on 15 April 1790[5] as a result of severe dysentery exposed his son Ranjit Singh to Sikh politics at an equally early age. Ranjit Singh was born on 13 November 1780 in the village Badrukha. At the time of his birth Mahan Singh was away at war. On hearing from a messenger that his wife had given birth to a son and had decided to name him 'Budh Singh' after his great-great-grandfather, Mahan Singh demurred and stated 'He will be called Ranjit', the name meaning 'the victor of battles'. Ranjit Singh suffered ill health at a young age, which left him with a pock-marked face and blind in the left eye. But this setback did not deter him, and at the age of fourteen he took part in his first battle.

In 1799, with the help of Sada Kaur, Ranjit Singh wrested Lahore, the capital city of the Punjab, from its three weak rulers Gujjar Singh, Lehna Singh and Sobha Singh.[6] The people of Lahore had become tired of the bad administration and rule in the city, and had voiced their grievances to Ranjit Singh. At nightfall, Ranjit Singh entered the city when the citizens threw open the city gates. He now controlled the capital and this was the start of his legendary conquest of the entire Punjab. In 1801 he was crowned Maharajah of Lahore, and made further acquisitions of the cities of Kasur and Kangra in the same year, followed by the holy city of Amritsar in 1805. The British East India Company thought it time to consult with Ranjit Singh over his future plans. An agreement of friendship was reached in 1806, followed by the Treaty of Amritsar three years later, whereby the border between the two powers would be the River Sutlej.

Towards the end of the 1830s, Maharajah Ranjit Singh suffered a series of strokes, which led to his untimely death on 27 June 1839. His reign quickly became a legend in Indian history and his son Kharak Singh was proclaimed the next Maharajah. But Kharak Singh was a weak king, lacking ambition and worldly sense, while his son Kanwar Naunihal Singh was a dashing and handsome young man who had always played a prominent part during his grandfather's rule, having pride of place in the royal court. The public admired him and his hatred for the British made him a favourite with the military. He shared the attitudes of his distinguished grandfather; groomed in warfare and military training, he was a natural ruler in the style of the 'Lion of the Punjab'. Kanwar Naunihal Singh did not approve of his father's ways and saw the weaknesses that the country was developing. On 8 October 1839, with the help of the Prime Minister Dhian Singh Dogra, Kanwar Naunihal Singh overthrew his father and brought the Punjab directly under his own control. However, it is interesting to note that during Naunihal Singh's rule he never made himself Maharajah – his father remained on the throne and was still called the Maharajah.

The Punjab enjoyed fine administration until late 1840 when Maharajah Kharak Singh fell seriously ill and passed away on 6 November. After cremating his father, Naunihal Singh was returning to the Lahore Fort when an archway in the north gate of the *Hazuri Bagh* mysteriously fell on him. The young prince suffered fatal injuries and was declared dead two days later.

Sher Singh, the second son of Ranjit Singh, put forward his claim for succession, but Naunihal Singh's wife Sahib Kaur was pregnant with the late prince's child. Rani Chand Kaur, the mother of Naunihal Singh, was made Regent until Sahib Kaur gave birth. The child was stillborn, however, and Rani Chand Kaur was forced to resign her regency, and was later murdered. Sher Singh, who now had the support of the Prime Minister, proclaimed himself Maharajah on 18 January 1841 with little opposition. The Sandhawalias, who were the cousins of the royal family, were outraged, especially as they did not acknowledge Sher Singh as the true son of Ranjit Singh. They had supported Rani Chand Kaur's regency and the recent intrigues at the Lahore court were too blatant. On 15 September 1843, the Sandhawalias took their revenge and assassinated Maharajah Sher Singh and his young son Prince Partap Singh. The Punjab was again in turmoil. The other sons of Ranjit Singh put forward their claims to the throne, but the Sikh Army supported the minor Duleep Singh.

The Parentage of Maharajah Duleep Singh and His Removal from the Punjab

Maharajah Duleep Singh's mother, Jind Kaur, was born in 1817 in the village of Chahar in the Sialkot district of the Punjab.[7] She was the eldest of three sisters and two brothers, the daughter of Manna Singh Aulakh, the kennel keeper for the palace at Lahore, in the service of Maharajah Ranjit Singh. Jind Kaur had grown to become an exceptionally beautiful young lady, coming to the notice of the old Maharajah at an early age. Her father would carry her on his shoulders and run beside the Maharajah's palanquin, suggesting that he assume the burden of his pretty daughter.[8] Manna Singh, however, was often regarded as a sort of buffoon.[9] The Maharajah was said to have been pestered day and night by Manna Singh, telling him that his daughter was the most beautiful creature in the world, whom he would give to the Maharajah as his wife so that she would make him young again.[10] The Maharajah agreed with Manna Singh once he had seen the charms of his blossoming daughter. They were married in 1835 by the ceremony of *karewa*, at her family village.

After the death of Maharajah Ranjit Singh in 1839, his beautiful widow Jind Kaur kept her distance from the durbar until her son Maharajah Duleep Singh was seated on the throne four years later. In 1843 Maharani Jind Kaur was appointed Regent, but in due course rumours of her illicit affairs and flirtations with her ministers also came to light, and her power began to slip. The Sikh Army was becoming increasingly powerful and out of control. In November 1845 the Maharani despatched the Sikh Army to the borders of the River Sutlej to confront the British, who were camped provocatively on the southern border. Unknown to the Maharani, her treacherous generals, Tej Singh and Lal Singh, had sold themselves to the British.[11] The leaderless Sikh Army fought on four fronts at Ferozeshah, Sobraon, Aliwal and Mudki. The British dealt them a crushing defeat, although the Sikhs were worthy opponents. The British entered the Punjab and the Treaty of Lahore was signed. Kashmir was to be sold off to pay the war indemnity and was purchased by Raja Gulab Singh. All territories between the River Beas and the River Sutlej were to be annexed, and the remainder of the Sikh Kingdom was to be administered by a 'Council of Regency' under the British resident Henry Lawrence.[12] The treaty was to remain in operation until Maharajah Duleep Singh attained the age of sixteen years, on 4 September 1854.

On 7 August 1847, during the inauguration ceremony for Tej Singh – who was to be made the 'Raja of Sialkot' by the British for services rendered in the first Sikh War – the young Maharajah Duleep Singh was ordered to place a saffron mark on the head of his treacherous general as a sign of blessing and confirmation. Just before the ceremony, Maharani Jind Kaur, who by now wielded no power in the durbar, told the Maharajah to refuse the gesture. Innocently the Maharajah did as his mother told him. The resident Henry Lawrence was not amused; he was by now finding the Maharani's attitude far too rebellious and threatening to British interests in the Punjab, and he ordered her to the Summan Tower of the Lahore Fort. 'As guardians of the boy we have the right to separate him at 8 years of age', wrote the Governor General Lord Hardinge,[13] who went on to inform Lawrence, 'There is sufficient justification on political grounds for separating the Prince from his mother at the present moment.'[14] The Maharani wrote from the Summan Tower to Lawrence, 'You have not done justice to me, you have kept no regard of the friendship of the Maharajah, you have caused me to be disgraced by other people. You have not even remained true to treaties and agreement.' The Maharani was indeed hard done by. 'Not even my allowance of one lakh and fifty thousand rupees has been paid to me. Why do you persecute us in this way, it is better that you hang us instead,' she added. 'Why do you take possession of the kingdom by under-hand means? Why don't you do it openly? On one hand you show friendship and on the other you put us in prison.'[15] Lawrence could no longer tolerate her presence in Lahore. On 19 August 1847, Duleep Singh was sent away from the palace, and on the same night the Maharani was removed from Lahore and incarcerated in the fort of Sheikhapura. She was transferred to Ferozepur on 15 May 1848.[16]

Meanwhile in the Punjab, suppression at the hands of the British had taken its toll. Two British officers, Vans Agnew and Anderson, were sent to Multan to take charge of the city from Diwan Moolraj, the Governor of Multan, a province in the Punjab. On the orders of Diwan Moolraj the Sikh soldiers rebelled and killed the two British officers, while at the same time Chattar Singh Atariwala, the Governor of Hazara, also rebelled in the Punjab.[17] His son Sher Singh Atariwala, who was a member of the Council of Regency, joined his father. The escalating situation suited the then Governor General of India, Lord Dalhousie, who allowed the rebellion to spread so that a large-scale offensive could be undertaken against the Sikhs for total annexation. After the subsequent battles of Ramnagar, Gujrat and Chillianwala, the Sikh soldiers surrendered at Rawalpindi. On 29 March 1849, Lord Dalhousie proclaimed the annexation of the Punjab and Maharajah Duleep Singh was deposed at the age of eleven and placed in the care of a Scottish army surgeon by the name of Dr John Login.

The deposed Maharajah became a ward of the British government and was completely isolated from his family and countrymen. Within five years of the annexation of the Punjab, the young Sikh monarch was transformed into a typical Christian gentleman and the teenage Maharajah was brought to England where his extraordinary journey in British society began.

An engraving of the Prince of Wales's visit to Maharajah Duleep Singh at Elveden Hall for a hunting party, published in the *Illustrated London News* in 1872.

An early panoramic view of the capital of the Punjab, Lahore, now in Pakistan, *c.* 1870. The photograph shows the tomb of Maharajah Ranjit Singh on the left and the Lahore Fort to the right. The tall tower is the minaret of the Badshahi Mosque.

1

The Birth of Duleep Singh

Maharajah Duleep Singh seated on his throne. A line engraving published in the Illustrated London News *in 1846, shortly after the close of the first Sikh War.*

During the monsoon season of 1838 in northern India, in between intervals of unbearable humidity, news of an imminent birth was filtering through to the East India Company stationed at its summer capital of Simla. On 4 September, with Maharajah Ranjit Singh's power at its zenith, amid loud chants of *Bole-so-nihal*, the birth of a son was announced. Guns were fired into the blue sky, and the firing of cannons saluted the seventh prince of the Punjab. Offerings were made from Nankhana to Nanded,[1] where hymns could be heard, and blessings from Hindu temples and Muslim mosques alike. The palace at Lahore was illuminated as if Diwali had come early. Sweetmeats and gifts were distributed around the city and the capital filled with nobility coming to welcome the lion's cub to the world.

The prince was born at the Lahore palace away from the Summan Burj where the senior Ranis of the Maharajah resided. The royal priest read from the Sikh scriptures and the name of Duleep Singh was derived.[2] A town in his name would soon follow.[3] Duleep Singh's mother Jind Kaur, the daughter of the palace kennel keeper, had lived her earlier life among the royal household and had married the ailing Maharajah just three years earlier. Words could not describe her beauty; she was the envy of all women and the dream of all men, but her neglect by a king who had so many wives and so many battles to fight had to be accepted. Maharajah Ranjit Singh had already secured his throne with a legitimate successor and cared little for the discreditable intrigues of his harem – although the astute Maharajah was never deceived, and he generally accepted the children as his own with a certain grim amusement.[4] On the news of a son the Maharajah expressed his pleasure but remained in Amritsar.[5]

But Ranjit Singh had fathered his last child and died following a stroke ten months later. Four years after that, on the death of Maharajah Sher Singh on 18 September 1843, Duleep Singh was proclaimed Maharajah aged just five years, with the help of his maternal uncle Jawahar Singh who wielded great influence in the Sikh durbar. He appointed himself prime minister in May 1845, while the now Maharani Jind Kaur was Regent. She took care of day-to-day administration while the infant Duleep Singh enjoyed the fruits of his position.

This period provided Duleep Singh with some of the best moments of his life. Surrounded by courtiers, he was attended with all the pomp of an Indian king. Adorned elephants and jewelled horses were at his beck and call, and troops of boys of his age were present for sharing his amusements. A horde of court physicians watched over his health, jumping at the slightest sign of a sneeze or a cough. His education was also maintained: besides instruction from the finest

The legendary 'Lion of the Punjab', Maharajah Ranjit Singh (1780–1839), founder and ruler of the Sikh Kingdom of the Punjab, *c.* 1850.

tutors of Persian and *Gurmukhi* in the land, he was taught how to ride, to fire a gun, and to use a bow and arrow. He showed great interest in wrestling, hunting and falconry, a hobby he would adopt later in life.

Following the defeat of the Sikh Army in 1846, the Maharajah was separated from his mother a year later. In 1849 the Sikh Army was totally defeated after an uprising and the kingdom of the Punjab was annexed to the British territories in India. The Maharajah was given a stipend of no less than £40,000 and no more than £50,000 per annum and placed in the care of a Scottish army surgeon, John Login. In November 1849 the then Governor General, Lord Dalhousie, decided to have the Maharajah removed from the Punjab, to the village of Fatehgarh.[6] There was much lamentation among the people, and loud cries of distress could be heard from the women as the Maharajah's cortège left the palace. He passed the tomb of his father, over which he whispered a silent prayer. The young deposed

Maharajah arrived at Fatehgarh on 19 February 1850, and later recalled how the local inhabitants showed sadness and sympathy towards him.[7] Most of his Punjabi servants were dismissed and replaced by locals. Shahzadah Sheo-Deo, a son of the late Maharajah Sher Singh, accompanied him along with the Shahzadah's mother Rani Dukhno.

The Maharajah's conversion was no secret. While Login had earlier written to his wife from Lahore, 'I cannot put the Bible in his hands yet,'[8] it seemed this was certainly on his agenda to be fulfilled at a more convenient date. While plans were being discussed for Duleep Singh's visit to England, Lord Dalhousie wrote to Login, 'If Duleep Singh is to go to England, let him be quietly baptised before he goes and by his own name of Duleep Singh'. In the summer of 1852 he was taken to the hill station of Mussoorie, where George Beechey painted him in oils.[9] The painting was later to be a parting gift to Lord Dalhousie. In Mussoorie Duleep Singh saw more European life and learned to play cricket with the English boys. He also became fond of shooting and walking. None of his influential Sikh countrymen were permitted to approach him, nor was he permitted to correspond with his mother. In fact he was cut off from all of his old associations.[10] With the replacing of his servants, many changes were taking place around him. His life-long Muslim companion was returned to the Punjab, while a Brahmin by the name of Bhajan Lal was appointed his confidential personal attendant. According to the Maharajah, Bhajan Lal was a Hindu in name only and had studied at one of the Mission schools at Farrukhabad. Maharajah Duleep Singh believed that in reality Bhajan Lal was acting as a spy on his movements and reporting to Dr Login.[11] Bhajan Lal gradually introduced Christianity to the Maharajah through the reading of the Bible. The Reverend James Kennedy of Benares was later to remark, 'what a striking fact! The young Brahmin tells his royal pupil of the water of life, and of its refreshing and life-giving qualities, but himself refuses to taste. The Brahmin directs the prince to the way of life and brings him to the gate, but himself shrinks back from entering. . . .'[12] The Reverend added 'He (Bhajan Lal) refuses to follow his pupils example. The Prince wished to take him in his suite to England. This would have led to the loss of caste, and the young Brahmin still refused.'[13] The reality was that Bhajan Lal was really a very religious Hindu and was employed to convert the Maharajah. Slowly the Maharajah began to show a desire to become a Christian. He wrote to Lord Dalhousie of how his attendant would read one or two chapters of the Bible to him every evening, and also informed Dr Login, 'You will be surprised to learn of my determination to embrace the Christian religion.'

Prince Duleep Singh in 1841, before he came to the throne. After his father's death, the young Prince Duleep Singh was left at the end of the royal pecking order. In 1841 he posed for the Hungarian painter August Schoefft,[14] who had been invited to Lahore by Dr Honigberger, the court physician, during the reign of Maharajah Sher Singh. This oil painting shows the three-year-old prince seated on a tree trunk with the Lahore Fort in the distance.

An *Illustrated London News* engraving of Maharajah Sher Singh leaning against a horse next to Ajit Singh Sandhawalia, 1843. Duleep Singh's status had faded considerably until that fateful morning in September 1843 when Ajit Singh Sandhawalia assassinated Maharajah Sher Singh. The young Duleep Singh was then proclaimed Maharajah and the history of the Punjab took a new turn.

The submission of the eight-year-old Maharajah Duleep Singh before the Governor General Sir Henry Hardinge on 19 February 1846, after defeat in the first Sikh War.

An early impression of Maharajah Duleep Singh and his mother the Maharani Jind Kaur, from *The Pictorial Times*, March 1846. The Maharani was much aggrieved at being separated from her son in 1847 following the defeat in the first Sikh War. Her appeals to Henry Lawrence fell on deaf ears. 'You are very cruel to me. You have snatched my son. For ten months I kept him in my womb, then I brought him up with great difficulty . . . I cannot bear the pain of this separation. Instead of this put me to death,' she pleaded.[15]

Fort Sheikhapura in the Punjab (now in Pakistan), showing the approach from the main gate leading to the inner quarters of the fort. The building on the left has beautiful Sikh murals and wall paintings. The Maharani was imprisoned here in 1847 for a year before being transferred to Ferozpur. In 1849 Maharani Jind Kaur was shifted to Fort Chunar, but on 18 April she escaped,[16] disguised as a slave girl,[17] arriving at Kathmandu ten days later. She had travelled 300 miles through the most populous parts of Bengal, and on her arrival all she asked for from the court at Nepal was to live at liberty under the protection of the Nepalese government. There she was not treated any better by Jung Bahadur, king of Nepal, who kept her as a 'practical prisoner, who grudged her every penny of the pension he said he allowed her'.[18]

The first photograph of Maharajah Duleeep Singh in 1848 by John McCosh, a surgeon with the East India Company. This early calotype shows a blurry but unique image of the ten-year-old Maharajah in his finery. During this period he was awoken and dressed by five personal valets, each of whom held a different suit, hand embroidered in the finest silks and velvets. He would then choose his dress for the day, before a large tray with the finest and most precious pearl necklaces, ruby rings and gold-and diamond-encrusted turban ornaments was brought in from the treasury from which he would select jewels for his daily attire.

Dr John Login. On 6 April 1849 Duleep Singh was formally introduced to his new guardian, John Spencer Login, a Bengal Army surgeon, whose salary of £1,000 per annum was to be paid from the Maharajah's pension.[21] John Login made the necessary arrangements for the Maharajah's education on reaching Fatehgarh in 1850. A tutor, Mr Walter Guise, was also appointed for the Maharajah, although he was later described by Dr Login as 'unsuitable'. On 8 March 1853 the Maharajah was formally admitted into the Christian faith. Reverend William James Jay conducted the service, while John and Lena Login, Colonel Alexander and Mr Guise signed the baptismal register as witnesses at the Maharajah's own house, as the church at the time was under repair. Also in attendance were around twenty Europeans and an equal number of the Maharajah's native servants.[22] Lord Dalhousie showed his satisfaction on hearing the news, and in a letter to his friend, Sir George Couper, on 12 March 1853 he wrote, 'This is the first Indian Prince of many who have succumbed to our power, or have acknowledged it, that has adopted the faith of the Stranger.'

Opposite: An early engraving of Maharajah Duleep Singh arriving at the British camp, after the defeat in the second Sikh War. On 30 March 1849, the terms of the annexation were read to Maharajah Duleep Singh. He was to resign for himself, his heirs and successors all right, title and claim to the sovereignty of the Punjab. All the property of the state was to be confiscated by the British government and the famous Koh-i-noor diamond to be surrendered to the Queen of England. He was allotted a pension of no less than four *lakhs* and not exceeding five *lakhs* of the Company's rupees per annum.[19] The only item to remain was the title of 'Maharajah Duleep Singh Bahadur', that too providing he remained obedient to the British government and resided at such a place as the government thought fit. The confiscated property was sold in eight public sales, called the 'Lahore Confiscated Property', and included such personal and sentimental items as the wedding garments of his grandfather, the plume of the tenth Sikh Guru – Guru Gobind Singh – and Maharajah Ranjit Singh's golden throne, as well as dishes, plates, cups and cooking utensils from the palace.[20]

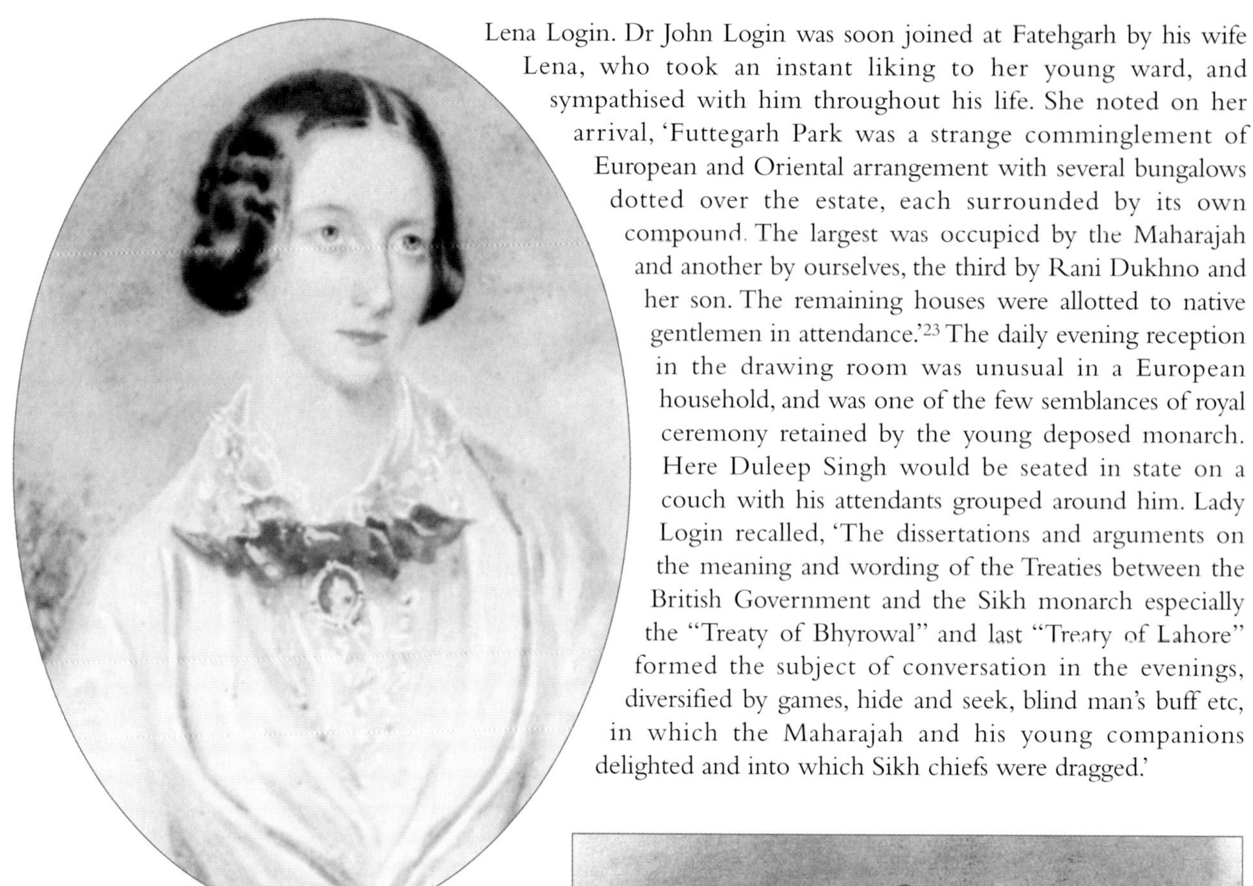

Lena Login. Dr John Login was soon joined at Fatehgarh by his wife Lena, who took an instant liking to her young ward, and sympathised with him throughout his life. She noted on her arrival, 'Futtegarh Park was a strange comminglement of European and Oriental arrangement with several bungalows dotted over the estate, each surrounded by its own compound. The largest was occupied by the Maharajah and another by ourselves, the third by Rani Dukhno and her son. The remaining houses were allotted to native gentlemen in attendance.'[23] The daily evening reception in the drawing room was unusual in a European household, and was one of the few semblances of royal ceremony retained by the young deposed monarch. Here Duleep Singh would be seated in state on a couch with his attendants grouped around him. Lady Login recalled, 'The dissertations and arguments on the meaning and wording of the Treaties between the British Government and the Sikh monarch especially the "Treaty of Bhyrowal" and last "Treaty of Lahore" formed the subject of conversation in the evenings, diversified by games, hide and seek, blind man's buff etc, in which the Maharajah and his young companions delighted and into which Sikh chiefs were dragged.'

Tommy Scott, photographed in later life. The Maharajah's circle of English friends began to grow. There were Frank and Charles, sons of Major Boileau, and little Robbie Carshore, while a young English boy called Thomas Scott was soon to become the Maharajah's best friend at Fatehgarh. All the boys remained friends with the Maharajah throughout his life, in particular young Tommy, who became a colonel in the British Army. Tommy served in India with the Indian Civil Service and supported the Maharajah's case even when the Maharajah left England on bad terms with the government. But the Maharajah promised Tommy that if ever they met face to face on a battlefield, he would give him the first shot!

2

Life in England

Maharajah Duleep Singh in 1856. An engraving from a photograph by O.G. Rejlander was published in the Illustrated London News, *which announced that the Indian Prince was visiting England.*

The question of finding a suitable bride for the Maharajah was high on Dr Login's list of priorities; after all he said, 'I am his "Ma-Bap",[1] and he trusts me to do what may be necessary for his happiness.' The Maharajah had been earlier engaged to the daughter of Chattar Singh Attariwala, the ex-Governor of Hazara, and a key member of the rebellion in the second Sikh War. In 1848 Chattar Singh had sent word to Lawrence of this alliance, which was politely ignored and the then British Resident Sir Frederick Currie refused to fix a date. Many likely candidates were sought including the daughters of the Raja of Coorg as well as the late Maharajah Sher Singh's widow. Duleep Singh declined every one. Lord Dalhousie, on the other hand, did not wish to countenance any relations henceforth between the Maharajah and the Sikhs, either by alliance with a Sikh family or sympathy with Sikh feeling.[2]

Dr Login began telling the Maharajah of the splendours of England and urged him to request permission to visit the land of his British masters. The Maharajah wrote to Government House, 'I am anxious to go and ready to start whenever his lordship gives me permission. I do not want to make a show of myself, but to study and complete my education, and I wish to live in England as quietly as possible.' The letter was obviously the clever design of Dr Login, who knew how to impress the 'Court of Directors' whose permission it would be necessary to obtain.[3] After one final summer trip to Mussoorie, where the Maharajah was painted in oils by George Beechey, the entourage headed towards England, after permission was granted on 21 January 1854.

On 19 April 1854 the Maharajah and his party set sail for England. Following Lord Dalhousie's directions they stopped and spent a few days in Cairo, playfully enjoying the Pyramids. Much to the horror of the Arab guides, Duleep Singh insisted on a race to the top of one of the monuments with his friends, while Ibrahim Pasha's carriage and equipage was placed at his disposal to view the sights. Dressed in his pearl necklaces, the Maharajah had now adopted a semi-European style of dress, and wore his native dress with all its splendid jewels only when he attended official engagements.[4] Lady Login recalled, 'He was never without his three rows of enormous pearls around his neck, and a pair of large emerald and pearl earrings.'[5] However, for the time being he kept his Sikh turban, protecting his long uncut hair. Being treated like a royal personage, he was semi-officially received at Malta, but did not land at Gibraltar. A full twenty-one gun royal salute was fired in his honour by the military authorities of both countries in recognition of 'the first Indian Prince to be acknowledged by the English Government'.[6]

In the month of May 1854 the Maharajah reached Southampton, and on his arrival at the capital he lodged at the prestigious Mivarts Hotel[7] where he was treated with the distinction proper to persons of exalted rank. Her Majesty Queen Victoria received him at Buckingham Palace on 1 July. Of this first visit she wrote '[he is] extremely handsome and speaks English perfectly, and has a pretty, graceful and dignified manner'. She added, 'I always feel so much for these poor deposed Indian Princes.'[8] The Queen decided that his rank was to be the same as that of a European prince, and as chief of the native princes of India he came next in precedence after the royal family.[9] He was even seated near Her Majesty in the House of Lords at the opening of parliament. His straightforwardness made him a favourite with Queen Victoria, and his outspoken comments on things in general seemed especially amusing to the Prince Consort, who even designed a coat-of-arms for the Maharajah, showing a lion standing beneath a coronet surmounted by a five-pointed star. The motto the Prince Consort chose was *Prodesse quam Conspici*, which ironically meant 'To do good rather than be conspicuous'. On ceremonial occasions the Maharajah proudly wore the 'Grand Cross Star of India' (GCSI), to which order he had been admitted in the very first list of recipients as a 'Knight Grand Cross' by the Prince Consort in 1861.[10]

In 1857, at the age of nineteen, the Maharajah asked to manage his own household. After some discussion the request was granted. His pension was increased to £15,000 per annum, although this fell far short of the minimum of £40,000 agreed in the Treaty of Lahore. The Maharajah noted 'that every circumstance connected with his early life was calculated to impress him. The appointment of a highly salaried officer of the Company as his guardian, the choice of companions, maintained at his cost, the control of his movements down to the minutest particular by the British Government.' The reason Lord Dalhousie gave for not allowing him to attend public school in England was that 'he might be thrashed'. Dr Login informed the Maharajah that the government considered it 'unbecoming his rank' to go to university. But later in life Her Majesty insisted on sending the Maharajah's sons to Oxford and Cambridge. All of these oppressing circumstances in his own words were nothing less than 'cruel mockery'.[11]

The Bible presented to Maharajah Duleep Singh. On leaving India the Maharajah had presented Lord Dalhousie with the painting by George Beechey. In return the Governor General sent a parting gift of his own, a beautiful large bound and clasped copy of the Christian Bible, inscribed 'To His Highness Maharajah Duleep Singh, this holy book, in which he had been led by God's grace to find an inheritance richer by far than all earthly Kingdoms, is presented with sincere respect and regard by his faithful friend, DALHOUSIE. April 5, 1854.'[12]

Maharajah Duleep Singh, by Franz Xaver Winterhalter. In 1854 the Maharajah sat for Winterhalter at Buckingham Palace: it was the Queen's desire to have a full-length picture of her favourite[13] (she even had a marble bust of the Maharajah made by the renowned Baron Marochetti in 1856)[14] and it was during one of these sittings for the painting that she placed the large Koh-i-noor diamond in his palm, and the Maharajah's eyes lit up. He had never dreamt of seeing the diamond again, and after a moment's thought he placed it back in the hands of the Queen, proclaiming, 'It is to me Ma'am the greatest pleasure thus to have the opportunity as a loyal subject, of myself tendering to my sovereign the Koh-i-noor.'[15] Dr Login informed Sir George Couper of this 'present' to Queen Victoria. When the news reached Lord Dalhousie, he called Duleep Singh's noble act 'arrant humbug'. Writing to Sir George Couper, Dalhousie added, 'It was nothing of the sort and he as well as I know it was nothing of the sort. If I had been within a thousand miles he would not have dared such a piece of trickery.'

The Maharajah at Osborne House, photographed by his German teacher Dr Ernest Becker, 23 August 1854.

Osborne House on the Isle of Wight. Maharajah Duleep Singh became a regular visitor to Windsor and to Queen Victoria's holiday home at Osborne House, befriending the royal Princes, the Prince of Wales[16] and Prince Alfred.[17] Correspondence with the Princes was strongly encouraged, while the Maharajah's particular favourite was little Prince Leopold, who suffered from haemophilia. Duleep Singh would carry him around on his back so that he would not fall and could keep up with the others.[18] The Queen took a keen interest in Duleep Singh's wellbeing, and personally recommended his teachers and professors, Professors Bentley and Becker for science and German, Dr Edward Rimbault and W.G. Cusins for music. The Maharajah learned to speak German, but Italian was his favourite, in which he was tutored by Signor Montanari.

The charismatic Maharajah photographed in London in 1856. His dashing looks and Indian appearance made him an ideal party accessory. He at once entered into the grand social circle of the nobility, and offers came in from all over England from hostesses wanting an exotic figure to enliven their parties. They went to great lengths to impress him, as Lady Login amusingly observed: 'At a dinner given by a General, the hostess pressed the Maharajah to take some curry she had especially made for him. She went on to say that no doubt it was very inferior to what he was accustomed to, but trusted in that case that he would honestly tell her if it was not good. The poor boy was politely endeavouring to swallow a little of the mixture which was very unlike an Indian curry; but when his hostess said this, he believed she meant it and putting down his fork and spoon with a sigh of relief, he said, "Oh, you are quite right! It is horrible! Take it away!" The hostess had apparently thought herself an authority on Indian dishes.'[19]

The Maharajah at Roehampton on 7 June 1856, photographed by Prince Albert Edward, the Prince of Wales. A house was taken at Wimbledon for the Maharajah by the East India Company and afterwards at Granard Lodge, Roehampton, for six months, after which time Ashburton Court was also secured for as long as he wished to stay in London. It was here at Roehampton that he made many noble friends, including the Earl of Leven, whose son Leslie Melville would later become his close aide. The Maharajah's wish to go to university was not permitted and this disappointment had an unfortunate effect on his studies.[20] He soon became tired of his life at Roehampton and asked to be allowed to return to India before the time originally fixed. To smooth matters and turn his attention elsewhere, the Board of Directors suggested a 'continental tour'. Dr and Lady Login took him to France and Italy on a four-month trip in December 1856. At Naples the Maharajah heard of the Indian Mutiny, which altered his plans of returning to India in the immediate future. He was informed that his residence in Fatehgarh had been ransacked and burnt down. As the Maharajah's visit to England was only meant to last a couple of years, much of his valuable property had been left behind in his *toshkanna*, in the care of his English steward, Sergeant Elliot.[21]

Castle Menzies in Scotland. On his return to England in May 1857, Sir John Login took this medieval castle in Perthshire on the Maharajah's behalf. It was here that the Maharajah became initiated into the sport of grouse shooting, entertaining many distinguished guests from India House, cabinet ministers and members of the opposition. At the urging of the Duke of Athol, a regular visitor at the shoots in Menzies, the Maharajah adopted a kilt for shooting on the moors in the Highlands, for which the Duke had suggested his own tailor. The Roehampton residence was still kept on.[22] At Castle Menzies Duleep Singh also became acquainted with Samuel Baker, an eccentric adventurer and patriotic enterpriser, who resided in Lochgarry House some 20 miles away.[23]

Mulgrave Castle in Whitby, Yorkshire. When the lease at Menzies expired, the shootings at Auchlyne House on Loch Tay were rented from Lord Breadalbane for a short time.[24] In May 1858, on the Maharajah's return from a shooting expedition in Sardinia, the lease at Mulgrave Castle was secured from Lord Normanby, Ambassador to Florence. Mulgrave was above the cliffs in Whitby and had a grouse moor with some excellent shooting. The Queen thought it best that a gentleman of some position should reside with the Maharajah during his first years of majority, to attend him at court and at state occasions, for which Colonel James Oliphant was selected.

An engraving of Princess Victoria Gouramma of Coorg, *c.* 1860. It was during this period that the question of marriage was again brought to the Maharajah's attention. The Queen tried her hand at matchmaking, selecting her thirteen-year-old goddaughter Princess Victoria Gouramma of Coorg, who earlier Dr Login had tried to match with the Maharajah in Fatehgarh. The Maharajah gave as his reasons for not marrying that he wished to see the world, and did not want to marry until he was aged twenty-three or twenty-four. Besides, he thought of the Princess Gouramma as a friend and not a wife. In 1858 the Queen announced that she had assumed the government of the territories of India administered by the East India Company. The Maharajah was now free to resume his intention of visiting India, although the real reason was to find his mother, who had escaped to Nepal in 1849.

Maharajah Duleep Singh in his Sikh turban over a semi-European dress, in 1859, in the first series of *The Drawing-Room Portrait Gallery of Eminent Persons* by the engraver D.J. Pound. The delightful collection of about forty engravings is principally from photographs by Mayall, and many are in Her Majesty's private collection.

3

Return to India & Marriage

Maharajah Duleep Singh, c. 1861. *An early carte-de-visite photograph of the Maharajah in his native dress by Henry Mullins*

In 1859 the Maharajah commissioned his long-serving native attendant, the *Pundit* Nehemiah Goreh, to travel to Kathmandu on his behalf, to find out at first hand how his mother was really living. Instead of going himself, the *Pundit* sent the Maharani a letter through a native banker visiting Nepal on business. But the letter was intercepted and came to the notice of the Viceroy, who forbade the *Pundit* to communicate with the Maharani except through the British Resident at Nepal,[1] Colonel Ramsay, who remarked, 'The Rani had much changed, was blind and lost much of her energy which formerly characterised her, taking apparently but little interest in what was going on.'[2] The Maharajah cleverly devised the idea of travelling to India for a cold-weather tiger shoot and at the same time to meet his mother. He arrived in Calcutta at the beginning of the year. In preparing for a season's sport, he had gone to great expense purchasing an India rubber boat, a swivel duck gun and all the latest inventions in rifles.

On 16 January 1861 the Maharajah met his mother at Spence's Hotel in Calcutta after thirteen and a half years apart.[3] It was an emotional reunion, and the Maharani had much to tell and ask her son. The Maharajah noted how she had become almost blind, not from age but from ill health aggravated by grief and disappointment, and he did not need to beg her to come with him to England: her private property and jewels were in the hands of the British government, who refused to restore them unless the Maharani chose to reside in a place outside India. They even offered to give her a pension of £3,000 per annum. He wrote to Lady Login, 'My mother has decided she will not separate from me any more, and as she is refused permission to go to the hills I suppose we shall return to England as soon as I can get passage.'[4] His trip had to be cut short, however, as Sikh troops, returning from the China War on ships from the River Hoogly, had heard the news of the Maharajah's arrival, and crowds began gathering with cries of 'Khalsa' outside Spence's Hotel. The authorities became alarmed, and Lord Canning requested the Maharajah to cancel the sporting trip and return to England with his mother.

On the passage home, the Maharajah suffered great seasickness while the Maharani bore the voyage well. He asked Dr Login to find a home for his mother in London so that on arrival the Maharani would have a place to stay, as it would take time to get all of her baggage and valuables safely landed. Dr Login found the Maharani a house at 'No.1 Round-the-Corner', Lancaster Gate in Bayswater, two doors away from the Login's residence.[5]

On Duleep Singh's return, his application for British citizenship was granted, and he completed the purchase of an estate in Gloucestershire which he had had his eye on before his trip to India.

The Maharani Jind Kaur, painted in oils by George Richmond *c.* 1862. In 1861, the Maharajah arrived back in England with his ailing mother. Lady Login observed that the Maharani was a far cry from her former self. 'The half-blinded woman sitting huddled on a heap of cushions on the floor, with health broken and eyesight dimmed, her beauty vanished, it was hard to believe in her former charms of person and conversation! However, the moment she grew interested and excited in a conversation unexpected gleams and glimpses and the torpor of advancing age revealed the shrewd and plotting brain of one who had been known as the "Messalina of the Punjab".'[6] The Maharajah tried to persuade his mother to move to Lythe Hall, but she would have none of it. In July 1861 he took her to Mulgrave Castle, where she stayed with him for a year, until he eventually found her her own place under the charge of an English lady at Abingdon House in Kensington.[7]

Hatherop Castle. In 1862 the government decided that the Maharajah should receive £25,000 per annum, with an immediate grant of £105,000 towards the purchase of Hatherop Castle in Gloucestershire, which cost altogether £183,000, the remaining amount being raised by a mortgage on the land purchased. The estate, although ideal for chasing fox, was not good for the conservation of game.[8] By 1863 the Maharajah was finding it unsuitable and already had his sights set on the Elveden estate in Suffolk, which had recently come on the market. The government sanctioned an advance of £110,000 at 4 per cent interest for the new purchase.[9]

The Maharajah Duleep Singh, *c.* 1863. Reunited after years of separation, mother and son passed their time reminiscing on the former glories and splendours of the Sikh durbar. The Maharani even had her son write to Dr Login about his ancestral lands at Pind Dadun Khan: she was using her trump card to have one last go at the British for what they had done. Even the Logins were sensing a dramatic change in the Maharajah's ways. Lady Login remarked that the Maharani was 'undoing much of the benefit of his English upbringing and tempting him to lapse into negligent native habit'.[10]

The wedding of the Prince of Wales and the Princess Alexandra of Denmark on 10 March 1863. This engraving from *The Graphic* shows his Royal Highness the Crown Prince of Prussia and his Royal Highness the Duke of Saxe-Coburg Gotha in their robes of the Garter standing next to the groom. The Maharajah attended this ceremony in St George's Chapel in his native dress, which gave zest to the occasion, leading the way for the other visiting Indian princes. The Maharajah took a prize seat among the royal family, and was also depicted lavishly in William Frith's painting[11] of this momentous occasion in his ornamental jewelled turban.

The Dissenters Chapel at Kensal Green cemetery. On 1 August 1863 the Maharajah sent a telegram to John Login at his Vernon Villa in Felixstowe, saying that his mother had died in London. The Maharajah had been at Loch Kennard Lodge, another of his hunting retreats in Perthshire. Dr Login arranged for the temporary housing of the Maharani's sumptuous white velvet-draped and jewelled coffin in the catacombs beneath the Dissenters' Chapel at London's Kensal Green, until such time as it could be taken to India for last rites. The simple ceremony was attended by a large contingent of Indian nobility. The nervous and often shy Maharajah gave a touching speech comparing the religion of his mother to the Christian faith. The Maharajah was inconsolable, but by her death the Maharani had already sown the seeds of discontent in Duleep Singh's mind, and these would influence his doings in later life.

The grave of Sir John Login at St Peter & St Paul, Church Street, Old Felixstowe. On 18 October 1863 the Maharajah was faced with the death of another parent, Dr Login, who had consoled him just two months earlier on his mother's death; so now there was no one to console him. The Maharajah had purchased Elveden Hall[12] just three weeks earlier and wanted to bury Dr Login in a new mausoleum which he proposed to build as a family burial site.[13] Lady Login, however, wished her husband to be buried at the Suffolk coastal town of Felixstowe.[14] The Maharajah obliged and built at his expense a rich red-granite and white-marble monument at his grave. The Maharajah now proposed to take his mother's remains to India, as it was the Maharani's last wish. Permission was granted in 1864, and Maharajah Duleep Singh made arrangements to travel, with a hidden agenda of his own.

A sketch of the young Bamba, *c.* 1862. Before leaving for India, the Maharajah wrote to the American Presbyterian school in Cairo to find a suitable good Christian wife. He had stopped off at Cairo on his first journey from India and had noticed the pretty pupils of the school there. He preferred to have a young and innocent girl, one he could train, educate and mould in his own way, rather than marry a woman of high rank. The Maharajah left for India on 16 February with his mother's remains, stopping briefly at the missionary school in Egypt. There he was instantly attracted to a petite sixteen-year-old called 'Bamba', who was extremely intelligent, having been teaching the younger children since the age of fifteen.[15] Bamba could speak only Arabic, and could communicate with the Maharajah only through an interpreter. The Maharajah proposed to her without delay, and she seemingly accepted without thought. Although it was agreed that he should carry out his filial duties in India first, he insisted that they should begin her training right away, by teaching her English, music and the art of etiquette to suit the social circle of the Maharajah.

Maharajah Duleep Singh's father-in-law, Otto Thomas Ludwig Muller. Bamba Muller was born in Cairo in 1847, and was brought up at the missionary school. She was the only daughter of Sophia, an Abyssinian lady, and Thomas Ludwig Muller, a German merchant banker and shipping merchant. Ludwig Muller was the only child of a German family, and was brought up by an adopted parent in Egypt.[16] It was during his time here that he became involved with Sophia.[17] A child was born out of wedlock whom they named Bamba. Ludwig was a married man and decided to place the baby at the local missionary school where he enabled Sophia to obtain employment as a teacher so that she could be close to their daughter.[18]

The Maharajah Duleep Singh, *c.* 1864. In the spring of 1864 Maharani Jind Kaur was cremated at Bombay, as the authorities would not allow her to be cremated in the Punjab. Her ashes were scattered in the River Godavari at Nasik (on the Panchvati side), where, on the left bank, the Maharajah erected a small *samadh* built as a memorial to his mother.[19] On leaving India, Duleep Singh wrote to his great friend Ronald Lesley-Melville that he 'had met a young lady at the mission school who would prove all he wished for as a wife'. Announcements were also sent to Lady Login and Mr Oliphant. His loved ones in England were not impressed; to go in search of a wife and carry out a courtship in the middle of a funeral voyage, then bring back the wife in place of the coffin, was seen as 'truly the acme of incongruous association'.[20]

The Maharajah in his wedding robes. After carrying out his mother's last rites the Maharajah returned to Cairo, where he married Bamba Muller on 9 June 1864. The groom was dressed in his finery, with his 'Grand Cross Star of India' insignia firmly mounted on his chest, over a semi-European dress and a ceremonial robe. A diamond-studded *kalghi* adorned his wonderfully pearled turban with jewelled and richly stoned necklaces entwined around his neck and across his shoulders. The bride was arrayed in European dress with short lace sleeves, and her hair was twisted into several long tight plaits hanging straight down, with a simple veil at the front. The ceremony was performed at Ludwig Muller's house, where Duleep Singh spoke his vows in English while the new 'Maharani' pronounced hers in a musical voice in Arabic.[21] The Maharajah took his new wife to Ramleh near Alexandria for about a month before heading to England.

The Maharani Bamba in 1864. On returning to England, one of the first people to see the new Maharani of Lahore was Mrs Leven, wife of the Earl of Leven. She was dressed in her native costume, in a full skirt and traditional Turkish jacket, while on her head was a jaunty cap made of large fine pearls, worn on one side with a long tassel of pearls hanging almost to her shoulder. Mrs Leven quickly wrote to Lady Login of her finds, 'She is remarkably nice looking, with very fine eyes and a sweet expression.' The obvious comparison was made to Queen Victoria's Indian goddaughter, Princess Gouramma of Coorg: 'she is better looking than Gouramma, and a size bigger,' she added; 'Bamba means pink, and she was pink till six weeks ago when she had jaundice.' The Maharajah was totally besotted with her, showing her off like a prized trophy to all his friends. He would fuss around her and minister to her slightest whim, even interfering in matters of attire, on which he had some absurd notions.

Loch Kennard Lodge, Perthshire. In the winter of 1864 the Maharajah brought his new bride here while the extensive renovations at Elveden Hall were being carried out. He installed a governess, Mrs Hart, on loan from the missionary school to teach the Maharani English and general knowledge. The Maharajah decided in the following year to enjoy some sunshine with his wife in Egypt, as the work at Elveden was taking longer than anticipated. The couple went sailing on the Nile, and then on to Fayum and Delta where Bamba did some missionary work, distributing Bibles and reading the gospel.

The grave of the Maharajah's firstborn at Kenmore Church, *c.* 1870. In the summer of 1865 when the Maharani was pregnant with their first child, the Maharajah decided to take her to Scotland to his hunting lodge so that she could relax and he could enjoy some sport. On 4 August 1865 the Maharani gave birth to a son, but tragically, the baby boy died the very next day. The funeral was a quiet one within the confines of the grief-stricken couple's household with some local servants, and was held in nearby Kenmore church.

4

The Suffolk Squire

Maharajah Duleep Singh, c. 1865. A carte-de-visite photograph from Germany of the Maharajah in his princely attire.

The Maharajah and his wife returned to their newly renovated home in Elveden, 2 miles west of Thetford, on the Norfolk-Suffolk border. Here the Maharajah indulged in his passion for hunting and shooting, and promoted the little known method of taking hares by hawking. There was plenty of open heathland and large fields well suited for this purpose. In 1870, when the war between France and Germany broke out, the entire stud of hawks belonging to the Champagne Hawking Club, which had an establishment of some twenty or more hawks, mostly peregrines, and two or three goshawks, was removed to Elveden Hall.[1] The Maharajah sent John Barr, a falconer, to Iceland, to bring back a large stock of falcons. At one time he had as many as thirty-five in his mews, and three or four of these were regularly trained to fly the big brown hares of which the Maharajah had so many on his estate. But disease played havoc with the beautiful falcons, which were ill suited to the damp English climate.[2]

Like his friend the Prince of Wales, the Maharajah had a flirtatious nature. His notorious visits to Paris were well documented, especially with the lovely Parisian courtesan Leonide Le Blanc, introduced to the Maharajah by the London socialite Julian Osgood. Duleep Singh also knew he shared the not so pretty but very pleasing Ninon de l'Enclos with admirers such as the Duc d'Aumâlle and the young Georges Clemenceau, both of whom she once had at her feet at the same time. All three knew of the others and they were not jealous – on the contrary they were rather amused.[3] Another of the Maharajah's lovers was the extraordinary beauty Laura Bell, the daughter of an Irish constable who began her life on the stage in Dublin. When she made her first appearance in London and Paris, painters and aristocrats alike admired her. Her Irish wit and feminine artifice also attracted the likes of the Marquis of Hereford and Prince Louis Napoleon.[4]

In the nearby villages, children of Elveden Hall employees were often crudely mocked for their obvious biological link with the Maharajah. The Maharajah was quickly building a list of illegitimate offspring from his conquests. The rumours were strong and undoubtedly the Maharani was aware of them: their echoes were heard all the way up to the Highlands.

In 1872, his friend Ronald Melville suggested the Maharajah turn his hand to politics. Melville got the Duke of Richmond to recommend the Maharajah for the Carlton Club[5] and, supported by Lord Walsingham and Lord Colville, he was elected on 17 March 1873. It was decided he would stand for the Tory seat against Gladstone's son at Whitby, an area in which he was very popular during his residence at Mulgrave Castle. The candidature would surely have been an embarrassment to the government, and Gladstone asked the Queen to persuade the Maharajah to drop his plans: the Queen still had great influence on her favourite, and the Maharajah did as he was told.

The Maharajah then turned his attentions to the London scene. He became a member of the Garrick, the Marlborough, the East India and the Oriental, but was rejected by Whites. Suddenly London became the centre of his passions. Fellow visitors to the Alhambra club noticed that 'the Maharajah Duleep Singh is found every evening at the Alhambra graciously accepting the homage of the houris in the green-room, and distributing 9-carat gimcracks with oriental lavishness'. Waving his fancy piece of jewellery the Maharajah would ask 'what nice little girl is going to have this?', thus attracting the cream of the Alhambra courtesans. Polly Ash, alias 'Miss Ashsted', a bit-part dancer at the Alhambra between 1879 and 1880, quickly came to the attention of the Maharajah, who took her into his care and provided for her every need: in no time he became quite obsessed with her.[6] 'Polly was not devoid of common sense and retired some time later to a sumptuous flat in Covent Gardens courtesy of the Maharajah and an annuity that survived the donor.'[7] Ponsonby was later to remark in correspondence to the Prince of Wales regarding the Maharajah's finances that 'there was another, a Miss Ashsted who he gave £3,000 a year to during his first wife's life'.[8] In 1883 Sir Owen Burne stated that the Maharajah had settled an annuity 'on a Miss Ash whom he has taken into his keeping'. His escapades with Polly Ash could not be kept a secret for long; his son Prince Victor questioned him about the subject upon taking leave from Eton, but the Maharajah denied it as 'stories untrue and unfounded'. In a letter to Prime Minister Gladstone in 1882, the Maharajah let the address of his love-nest slip: 'I shall not return to town till Monday next when my certain address always is 34 King Street, Covent Garden, where I go to write the music of my opera every day.'[9] The Maharajah was soon to get bored with Polly Ash, however, sweeping her aside with the arrival of a new playmate whose identity was to create a certain mystery. The Maharajah now supported on his arm a younger and prettier girl, a chambermaid from Cox's Hotel, a sleazy, notorious gentleman's playground at 54/55 Jermyn Street – and the chambermaid would play a leading role later in the Maharajah's life.

Elveden Hall before the Maharajah's renovations, *c.* 1860. The Georgian country house of Admiral Keppel and latterly of the sporting squire William Newton was redesigned fit for an oriental king. Work began immediately after its purchase, and was executed under the superintendence of the architect Mr John Norton of Cubitt and Co. from Grays Inn Road, London.

Opposite: Drawing room at Elveden Hall, *c.* 1870. The Maharajah rebuilt the structure in red brick and ancaster stone, dressing it in an Italian style. He desired the interior of the house to be reminiscent of the fine Mughal palaces he was accustomed to in his earlier years. The house was to be his very own kingdom. Indeed, it was especially designed to accommodate his sporting habits, taking full advantage of its fine game surroundings. During this period the Maharajah acquired the vast portrait collection by the Hungarian artist August Schoefft[10] who had painted the young Duleep Singh at Lahore in 1843. The art collection adorned the high walls of the Hall. The enormous 'Court of Lahore' scene was hung in the dining-room with Captain Goldingham's portrait of Duleep Singh.[11] The Maharajah also commissioned a painting of himself, an exact copy of the Franz Xaver Winterhalter portrait commissioned by Queen Victoria in 1854.[12]

The aviary at Elveden, *c.* 1870. At the rear of the Hall an aviary was built to house exotic carrion birds, from Indian hawks to Icelandic gerfalcons. Golden pheasants would be seen sitting on the lawns beneath the cedars among the parrots, peacocks and buzzards from Holland. There were even tales of apes and a kangaroo at Elveden.

The old church of St Andrew in Elveden before its extension, *c.* 1865. The church of St Andrew on the Elveden Estate was also restored and extended by the Maharajah in 1869, with a vestry to the north of the chancel, a priest's door on the south side and the windows of the nave renewed in Bath stone. Lord Iveagh further extended the church in 1904 to its current size, adding the new nave and chancel dedicated to St Patrick; thus it became the church of St Andrew and St Patrick.

Prince Victor Duleep Singh photographed at Bury, *c.* 1868. After settling into their lavish Elveden estate, Duleep Singh and Maharani Bamba decided to try for another child. In the summer of 1866 the Maharani gave birth to a healthy boy whom they named Prince Victor in honour of the Queen. The Maharani was soon kept busy with the arrival of another child, Prince Frederick, in 1868. The house suddenly began to fill with children as three daughters and a son followed – Princesses Bamba, Catherine and Sophia, and Prince Edward Albert.

A carte-de-visite photograph of the Maharajah in his Sikh attire, *c.* 1870. The Queen had always intended to make the Duleep Singhs English in all except name, so she sent the Duke of Argyll, the Secretary for India, on a special mission to offer peerages to both princes, a marquisate for Prince Victor and an earldom for Prince Frederick. The Maharajah, however, replied, 'I thank Her Majesty most heartily and humbly convey my esteem, affection and admiration. Beyond this I cannot go. I claim myself to be royal; I am not English, and neither I nor my children will ever become so. Such titles – though kindly offered – we do not need and cannot assume. We love the English and especially their monarch, but we must remain Sikhs.' He walked across to a table in the great library at Elveden and opened a drawer. 'This,' he said, drawing out some paper, 'is the design for my coat-of-arms, drawn up by the Prince Consort and initialled by the Queen. I use them out of courtesy to Her Majesty, but will not register them at the College of Arms. I am not English.'[13] The Duke later remarked he had never seen truer dignity or more real independence of spirit.

Opposite: Hookum Singh standing outside Elveden Hall, *c.* 1865. The Maharajah loved showing his generosity, especially to his employees, and at Christmas time a pair of rabbits would be sent to each household. He and his family would also join estate workers for barn parties. One of the gamekeepers recalled, 'A notable event would be a party and sports held at Chamberlains Hall Barn, Eriswell. The great barn was warmed by turf fires on the earthen floor. I can recall seeing the Maharajah Duleep Singh, the Maharani and their two sons Prince Victor and Prince Frederick at one of these frolics. His Highness . . . laughed heartily at the unsuccessful attempts to climb the greasy pole, at the top of which a sovereign had been placed.'[14]

Hookum Singh and Aroor Singh, *c.* 1870. Locally, the Maharajah became known as the 'Black Prince' – not in a distasteful manner, but more in an affectionate way. Maids, valets, butlers, gardeners and gamekeepers were employed and suddenly the sleepy village of Elveden was brought to life. Two Sikh valets, Hookum Singh and Aroor Singh, were also engaged, the latter of whom would stay by the Maharajah's side for years to come.

The Maharajah Duleep Singh at a shooting party with the Prince of Wales, at Elveden, *c.* 1875. Standing from left to right are Lord Frederick Fitzroy, Lord Rendlesham and the Earl of Leicester. Seated are Sir Reginald Beauchamp, an unidentified gentleman, the Prince of Wales, General Sir Jas MacDonald and Maharajah Duleep Singh. By now the Maharajah had become famous for his shooting skills and was among the top shots in the country after the Prince of Wales, who was a regular visitor to the Elveden estate. Guests arrived from all over the country for the grand hunting parties here, including the Lords Ripon, Leicester, Henniker, Holmestead, Beaumont, De Grey, Stradbroke and Buxton, and the Duke of Athol.

Opposite above: Royal hunting party at Elveden, December 1876. From left to right, standing, are Lord de Grey and Lord Holmestead. Seated are Lord Powercourt, Lord Beaumont, the Prince of Wales, Lord Stradbroke and Lord Ripon. Sitting on the ground are the Duke of Athol and Maharajah Duleep Singh. On his visit in 1876 the Prince of Wales wrote, 'We had the most extraordinary good days shooting having killed yesterday and today close on 6000 head, nearly 4500 of which were pheasants! It is certainly the most wonderful shooting I ever saw, and I doubt whether such bags have been ever made before.'[15]

Opposite below: Royal shooting group at Heveringham Hall, 22 November 1876. Duleep Singh held two records. On 8 September 1876 he bagged 780 for 1,000 cartridges expended, rated as the largest bag ever made by one gun in England;[16] and he claimed 440 grouse to his own gun at the Perthshire estate at Grundtually.[17] The Maharajah is pictured here at the seat of his friend, the Right Honourable Lord Huntingfield. From left to right are Sir Hugh Cholmeley, General Sir Jas MacDonald, HRH the Duke of Cambridge, Col J.C. Vanneck, Lord Colville, Col Bateson, Maharajah Duleep Singh and Lord Huntingfield.

Ladies' tennis party at Elveden in November 1876. The ladies too had their parties. The wives of dukes, earls and lords would enjoy the grand feasts at Elveden over the latest pieces of aristocratic scandal and gossip, in the company of their hostess the Maharani Bamba, while indulging in a bit of tennis. The parties always ended with a fine group photograph of all the distinguished guests. Left to right, standing are Miss J. Angerstein, Mr Bishop, Miss Oliphant, Mrs Oliphant, Col Oliphant (the Maharajah's equerry). Seated in the middle row are Lady Dacie, Lady Boileau, Maharani Bamba Duleep Singh, Lady Cotteral, Mrs Angerstein. Sitting at the front are Prince Frederick, Prince Victor and Miss Angerstein.

Opposite above: The ladies' party at Elveden, December 1876. A gathering in the rear garden of Elveden Hall on the same occasion as the royal hunting party. From left to right, standing, are Miss Helen Henniker, Lady Beaumont, Lady Stradbroke and Lady Buxton. Seated are Mrs Oliphant, Lady Powercourt, Maharani Bamba Duleep Singh, Dowager Lady Henniker and the Duchess of Athol. Seated on the floor is Miss Henniker with Lady Augusta Rose.

Opposite below: Maharajah Duleep Singh standing at the entrance to the Hall, *c.* 1875. Elveden was to become a sportsman's paradise. Partridges were hand reared, being fed on rice, rabbits and eggs, together with a special kind of meal originated by the Maharajah's head gamekeeper, Mr James Mayes.[18] 'The Maharajah was also very fond of shooting driven rabbits and had some platforms built a few feet up certain trees where they commanded some open places which were specially cleared and over which the rabbits would have to run. Apparently the smell was lost by the guns being a few feet up.'[19] Duleep Singh also held the warren near Elveden Hall on a 99-year lease, one provision being that the ground must not be broken. He had trees planted around Warren Lodge to provide shelter, and in consequence an action was brought against him for breaking the ground. However, the Maharajah successfully defended himself and rabbit digging was afterwards done on a large scale.[20] After a hard day's shoot all surplus hares, rabbits, pheasants and whatever else slaughtered at Elveden Hall was rounded up by the estate gamekeepers and despatched to Baily the poulterer in Mount Street, London, for a shilling a head.[21]

The ladies' party at Elveden, December 1877. From left to right, standing, are Lady Fitzroy, Lady Leicester, Mrs Oliphant, Lady Henniker and hiding behind the pillar is the Maharajah's equerry Col Oliphant. Seated are Lady Mary Coke, the Duchess of Athol, Lady Mildrid Coke, Maharani Bamba Duleep Singh, Miss Fitzroy and Lady Dacie. At the front are the young Princes Frederick and Victor Duleep Singh.

The Maharajah standing between close sporting friends, Elveden, October 1876. Lords Huntingdon and Walsingham both owned prime sporting estates of their own, to which Duleep Singh was often a visitor. Lord de Grey, one of the finest shots in the country, sits on a cushion.

Maharajah Duleep Singh, *c.* 1870. Tom Turner, later a gamekeeper at Elveden, recalled, 'I remember seeing the Maharajah partridge-shooting on the three-cornered field that runs to the left from the Eriswell crossroads to the blacksmiths shop at the beginning of Eriswell village. It was in 1875 and I was a small boy of seven. These were the days of muzzle-loaders and the Maharajah had three double-barrelled guns, and two loaders, who with their blue and green coats and waistcoats, powder flasks and leather shoot-bags, made a great impression on my mind.' The Maharajah purchased and rented several fields and hunting grounds around his estate, each for its own individual use. One such ground was at Wangford: 'I saw a good bag of partridges at Broom House, Wangford where the Maharajah attempted to kill 1,000 partridges to his own gun.'[22]

In 1879, the Maharajah Duleep Singh attended the marriage of his childhood friend Prince Alfred the Duke of Connaught to Princess Louise Margaret of Prussia, at Windsor Castle. This engraving from the *Illustrated London News* faintly shows the Maharajah standing at the far left behind the King of the Belgians and Prince Frederick Charles of Prussia. Standing to the right of the groom are Queen Victoria, Princess Beatrice, the Prince of Wales, the Duke of Edinburgh, the Princess of Wales and the Crown Prince of Prussia.

Opposite above: The Maharani Bamba and the Princess of Wales arriving at Elveden Hall in a horse-drawn carriage during the royal family's stay in 1876.

Opposite below: '*Hush!* (*The Concert*)' by Jacques Tissot, 1875. The Maharajah can be seen here sitting bareheaded behind his Indian valets Hookum Singh and Aroor Singh. Duleep Singh loved the London high-life, and would often be seen playing cards at the Union Whist Club in Jermyn Street, conveniently called the 'shirt shop', or enjoying discreet and illegal games of baccarat in the dark backrooms of west London. He was an excellent whist player among such admitted champions as Goldingham, Dupplin and Cavendish. He often spent the afternoons at the Marlborough or the East India, damning his partner if he ignored his 'call for trumps', while the evenings were spent at his favourite theatre, the Alhambra in Leicester Square, a moderate haunt for lovers of the can-can and ballet.[23]

Maharani Bamba holding Princess Sophia, with Prince Victor standing behind her and Prince Frederick, Princesses Catherine and Bamba seated on cushions, at the rear of the Hall, *c.* 1876. The Maharajah's extravagant lifestyle became a burden upon his finances. He had already incurred the huge cost of renovating Elveden, and now bringing up six royal children was not cheap. He continued his pressure on the government for an increase to his pension as stipulated in the Treaty of Lahore, but the reply was that the amount he received was sufficient. Duleep Singh followed up with two letters to *The Times* pleading his case for a settlement.[24] There was no one to turn to for help, as all the figures concerned in his controversial dethronement such as Login, Dalhousie and Hardinge had since departed and the current members of the board had no sympathy for him. They offered him advancements and loans, but he demanded an increase in his pension. The Queen declared she was helpless. Anxiety about his future was exacerbated by his responsibility to his heirs, and he soon began feeling dejected and disillusioned by his surroundings and began to search for ways to get himself heard and for justice to prevail.

Opposite left: Maharajah Duleep Singh and Maharani Bamba, *c.* 1870. With the poor farming season and agricultural depression of the late 1870s, revenues were at an all-time low and debts were mounting for the Maharajah. His relationship with the Maharani became sour, with frequent arguments over finances and his affairs. Earlier, during the Indian Mutiny of 1857, Duleep Singh's residence at Fatehgarh had been ransacked and looted, and he had lost much of his property, worth around £25,000. Following the Queen's proclamation of 1858, the Maharajah requested that 'he might be at least indemnified for this loss'. For some years there was no response from the government, which then offered him the sum of £3,000. Duleep Singh felt this amount inadequate and declined to accept it.[25] In 1879 the government of India advised that the 'obviously desirable course to adopt is the sale of the estate'. His mother had already apprised the Maharajah as to the vast amount of personal wealth and land which had been taken from him. The Maharajah now began looking into his family's large private estates and properties in the Punjab, which he had inherited from his father and which were not state property. He felt it was time to challenge the government about his landed property which had been illegally confiscated along with state property in 1849.

Right: Maharajah Duleep Singh, *c.* 1880. In 1881 the Maharajah rented 53 Holland Park in Kensington at £350 per annum, so that he could be close to the British Library to research the Punjab and its annexation. The result was an offensive publication titled 'Annexation of the Punjaub (*sic*)', brought out with the help of Major Evans Bell, a 'professional agitator' who stated that the revolt in Multan, which led to the second Sikh War, was allowed to escalate and could have been put down immediately. He described Dalhousie as 'a violator of treaties who abused the sacred trust and threw away the grandest opportunity ever offered to the British Government of planting a solid and vital reform up to the northern limits of India'.[26] The book was met with great opposition and was criticised for its inaccuracies, which the Maharajah was later obliged to amend. The government agreed to pay him an interest-free loan of £57,000, including previous advancements, to pay existing debts, but on the condition that the Elveden estate was to be sold on his death. The Maharajah argued the case: how could he secure his children's future if they were not to have their home when he died?

Duleep Singh, *Vanity Fair,*[27] 1882. As the Maharajah became excessively overweight, Donald Shaw, a prominent personality of 1860s London from the Maharajah's Alhambra days, crudely remarked, 'It was only when his Highness assumed evening dress that visions of Mooltan, Chillianwallah and Goojerat faded from one's brain, and a podgy little Hindoo seemed to stand before one, divested of that physique and martial bearing with either warriors or Sikhs, and only requiring as it were, a chutnee-pot peeping out of his pocket to complete the illusion.'[28] The Maharajah wrote to the government in 1882 asking permission to visit India. 'As I am now a naturalised Englishman, there is no legal difficulty to my going to the Punjab in order to obtain the requisite information which I can procure in no other way, regarding my private landed property.' The Viceroy was informed at Simla, he replied 'the Maharajah cannot be allowed to visit the Punjab . . . a large number of Ranjit Singh's devoted still survive and appearance among them of Ranjit Singh's son would probably have most disquieting effect.[29]

Thakur Singh Sandhawalia, the Maharajah's cousin (seated in the centre), with his sons Narinder Singh, Gurbachan Singh and Gurdit Singh, before leaving for England in 1884. In 1883 the Maharajah had commissioned his cousin to send in a report about his landed estates in India;[30] this he did on 9 November 1883. The Maharajah, in turn, published a narrative for private circulation, 'Duleep Singh and the Government', where he outlined his case sympathetically and sent it to all interested parties of high rank. It was a personal account of his treatment and experiences from his earliest recollections. Accompanied by his son, Narinder Singh (who was travelling under the false name of Gurmukh Singh) and two brothers, Gurdit Singh and Partab Singh[31] (a Sikh priest), Thakur Singh began telling the Maharajah of his ancestral past, as his mother had done twenty years earlier, while Pratab Singh would recite the *Guru Granth Sahib* to the Maharajah every evening. The Sikh entourage moved down to the Suffolk estate, where mischievous turbaned Sikhs could be seen moving around the hall, plotting the fall of British rule in the Punjab.

5

To Europe

Maharajah Duleep Singh, c. *1885, photographed before he left England in 1886.*

The Maharajah had now decided that he would go to India and leave England for good. He planned his departure for 16 December 1885, informing the government of his reason, which was 'to provide my family with such a home in India as shall not be sold at my death'. He further added his wish to visit Abchal Nagar[1] when reaching India, where he would be re-initiated into the Sikh faith.[2] But preparations needed to be made, such as the sale of his belongings, so the journey was put back. He also requested that specific amounts be deducted from his stipend and paid regularly to Lady Login, Mrs James Oliphant and others named by him. The government replied that he may reside only in the south of India at the presidency of Madras at Ootacamand. The Maharajah agreed. On his last interview with Sir Owen Burnes on 24 March 1886, the offer of a £50,000 settlement was referred to by the Maharajah as a 'paltry sum'. The Maharajah claimed he 'was not in debt and wanted no money, he was resolved to go to India and on no account whatever would he sign any paper either in renunciation of his claims or binding him never to return to his own country'.[3]

Maharajah Duleep Singh left England from Gravesend on 31 March 1886 in the P&O Steamer, SS *Verona*, with his wife and six children. A Sikh attendant, an Indian servant, a European nurse and an ayah accompanied them.

On 18 April 1886, however, a warrant was issued at Simla by the British government 'on the ground that it is necessary for the security of the British Dominion from internal commotion'. Similar warrants were also issued under the names of his wife and children. The steamer arrived at Aden on 21 April and the British Resident, Brigadier General Hogg, entered the ship and halted the Maharajah, who was dressed in his Sikh regalia. His family and fellow passengers looked on in shock. The Resident was careful not to use the word 'arrested', but the Maharajah would not leave the ship unless he was officially arrested. The Resident tapped the Maharajah on the shoulder and, after announcing to the passengers that there would be a 'great state trial', he left the ship to great cheers from the passengers. The family was housed at the British Residency pending further instructions from Simla, India's summer capital. In the meantime the Maharajah was allowed neither visitors nor communication with the outside world. The Resident was informed by the government that 'If the Maharajah desires to go back to England, he may be allowed to do so in an English ship on giving solemn pledge in writing that in consideration of his release from his present detention he will not renew his attempt to return to India'. The Maharajah would not agree to these terms: signing away his right ever to enter

India would be a tragedy and mean exile. He was advised to return to England, but instead he sent his family back on 6 May 1886. Two days later another relative, also Thakur Singh,[4] the son of Jawahar Singh of Wagah, visited the Maharajah accompanied by a fellow Sikh: they were allowed to see him in the presence of a British officer. On his cousin's arrival, Duleep Singh had a telegram sent to the Viceroy at Simla stating that 'I desire to take advantage of my cousin's presence here to be re-initiated into Sikhism'.[5] The Lieutenant-Governor informed the Foreign Secretary at Simla that 'Refusal would be misunderstood and might cause irritation as interference with freedom of religious conviction, it would also magnify his importance'. He added 'as long as he does not return to India consent will do little if any harm'.[6] And so, on the morning of 25 May 1886, Duleep Singh was re-initiated into Sikhism by the ceremony of *Pahul*, in the presence of Thakur Singh. The other four Sikhs were Aroor Singh of Kohali, Jawan Singh of Barki and two Sikhs from a transport ship, which then happened to dock at Aden.[7] The Maharajah became ill towards the end of May owing to excessive heat. The local doctors, Dr Jackson and Dr Harry, reported a weak heart, advising an early change to a cooler climate. The Resident was concerned: 'The Maharajah is better. Perhaps your Excellency may authorise me to let His Highness go to Europe unconditionally in case of serious illness.'[8] It would have been damaging for the government's credibility if Duleep Singh had died while under arrest. The Viceroy agreed. On 30 May the Viceroy informed the British Resident at Aden to 'let the Maharajah go to Europe unconditionally, but give him to understand in as gentle a term as you can that if he comes to India we shall be forced to take very decided steps'.[9]

The Maharajah left Aden in June 1886 heading for France, and on arrival he met Ada Wetheril.[10] Ada was the Cox's Hotel maid the Maharajah had been associated with in London, the mysterious lady he had left poor Polly Ash for some years earlier. Reacquaintance in Paris with Julian Osgood, a minor playwright and socialite of the Maharajah's Alhambra days, shed some fascinating light on Ada Wetheril, proving that the Maharajah knew her well before coming to France. In Osgood's memoirs, published some years later, he noted, 'I accepted a loan of money from the fair and aristocratic looking "Marini" the *Chère amie* of Duleep Singh and originally a chambermaid at a hotel in Knightsbridge'.[11] The money was to attend the Jubilee of the Grand Duke of Baden. He recalled that 'The Prince was so much in love with her that she had to send a wire twice a day to Elveden to tell him how she was getting on.' In late September 1886 Osgood bumped into the Maharajah and the same 'Marini' in Paris while staying at the same Dieppe hotel. Ada's name was not to be confused: 'Marini' was simply a corruption of 'Maharani' – she was the one that Duleep Singh called his queen. Julian Osgood remarked 'Marini looked like the typical "*Clara Vere de Vere*" the patrician English girl, the descendant of countless Earls, but when she spoke the charm vanished,' he added. 'Her manners were admirable, but her voice had the unmistakable Whitechapel accent, and her pronunciation and the expressions she used were, to say the least abnormal.' Osgood could be forgiven for mistaking Whitechapel for the Kennington-born Ada, but his perception of Ada's character was largely accurate.

Maharajah Duleep Singh, *c.* 1885. The Maharajah left Aden on 3 June 1886 with broken health, and arrived in Marseilles on the French mail steamer SS *Natal*. From there he headed for Paris, arriving at the Gare de Lyon the following day, and took up temporary residence at the Grand Hotel de St James et Bristol. He opened a mailbox and depository at the bank of Messrs Mallet Frères. On 7 December 1886 he received a letter from Robert Watson, an old friend from his Mulgrave days, which pressed him to return and push for a public trial. The Maharajah replied, 'No Watson I have done with the British Government forever and by the help of god my father I will for once at least overthrow the tyrannical, immoral and unscrupulous administration of India.' Then he announced his legendary plan: 'Let Russia give me only 10,000 men to appear on the North-West Frontier of India and the thing is done. For there are some 45,000 of the Punjabis, my former subjects in the British Army at this moment who would come over to me at once, and when other British troops would be sent to oppose me then the whole of the Punjab would rise in their rear.'[12] He also made his views clear to his cousin Thakur Singh, whom he now appointed as his prime minister.

Mikhail Katkov, the Maharajah's Russian guide, *c.* 1887. During December 1886 and the following January the Maharajah stayed at the Hôtel de Londres et New York in rue St Honoré, Paris, awaiting further instructions from his now favoured new assailant Patrick Casey. Casey was an Irish revolutionary who had been involved in a plot to dynamite Queen Victoria. He was lying low in Paris when the news of Duleep Singh's arrival reached him. Casey introduced him to the Russian journalist Katkov, who had internal connections and influence at the imperial court in Russia. Katkov became very close to the Maharajah, much to the dislike of the British government.

Elie de Cyon, 1890. Another conspirator Casey introduced to the Maharajah in the summer of 1887 was Elie de Cyon, a Russian Jewish-born doctor and journalist who was the Paris correspondent for the *Moscow Gazette*.

General Charles Carroll-Tevis. Unknown to Duleep Singh, around May 1887 a British spy had been firmly planted within the confines of his household in Paris. The spy was an ex-US Army cavalryman, General Charles Carroll-Tevis,[13] who had been handpicked for the job.[14] He was placed as a trusted member of the Fenian Brotherhood in Europe and unknowingly the Irish revolutionaries would recommend the double-crossing agent as a sidekick for the Maharajah. At a grand party held on 27 February 1887 by Madame Adam, a patriot and distruster of all things English, many of the Paris underground were present including Casey, Tevis, Cyon and the newly enrolled Maharajah.[15] Tevis would later ask Elie de Cyon to introduce him to the Maharajah.[16] From now on, the Maharajah's every visitor, correspondence and conversation would be conveyed to the Foreign Office in London. This vast number of intelligence reports would be filed discreetly under 'our correspondent', to conceal the informant's identity. General Tevis immediately reported back to London that he had discovered where Duleep Singh was residing in Paris and that he had a young English girl by his side. The girl was none other than Ada Wetheril.

Opposite: The Maharajah parading as Pat Casey with Katkov, 1887. *Punch* magazine mimicked the pair, with Katkov as the Russian bear playing the flute and Duleep Singh dancing to his tune. The Maharajah put his plan into action and, through Katkov's connections in the imperial court, he wrote to Tsar Alexander III: 'I endeavour to bring myself to Your Imperial Majesty's recollection, for doubtless sire, you cannot but have forgotten so humble an individual as myself, though I had the honour of being presented to Your Imperial Majesty by the Prince of Wales when Your Majesty visited England now many years ago.' Indeed the Maharajah had been introduced to the Tsar in England in May 1874. He continued, 'Therefore it is sufficient for me to state here that I am an unfortunate Indian prince, one of the monuments of British injustice, and earnestly implore you, sire, to find a safe asylum in Your Imperial Majesty's dominions as one of your most loyal subjects.' He offered his allegiance, adding that he required no pecuniary gain as his loyal subjects had furnished him with sufficient funds.[17] The letter was duly duplicated by Tevis and sent to London, while the Maharajah and Ada left for Russia on 17 March 1887 via Marseilles. They assumed the names Mr and Mrs Reginald Lorraine, under which identities they had their passports made out, and the Maharajah even used the name of Patrick Casey to disguise himself from the British authorities who he knew were spying on him. But who the spy was remained a mystery to him.

Maharani Bamba Duleep Singh, *c.* 1880. The embarrassed Maharani returned to England in May 1886, staying temporarily with her children at Claridges Hotel, and then moved on to their old London residence at Holland Park. The India Office agreed a pension for the family, the sum of £6,300 a year for Maharani Bamba, and £2,000 each for the eldest sons, while the Queen was kept informed of the children's welfare. The Maharani became withdrawn and very lonely, as many of her earlier so-called friends from the gentry had abandoned her because of her husband's antics. At Queen Victoria's Jubilee celebrations she was insulted by some women who referred to her as 'the thief's wife'. This was to be the final straw. The Maharani completely withdrew from public life and isolated herself from society. She packed Prince Victor off to Sandhurst and Prince Frederick to Eton.

The distressed Maharani Bamba. The Maharani's health continued to decline, but if the added pain from a skating accident[18] eight years earlier did not finish her, Duleep Singh's actions surely would. She never really recovered and became difficult to live with: her nanny, Miss Date, resigned her post. On 17 September 1887 her youngest daughter Princess Sophia caught typhoid. The Maharani prayed beside her little girl then she herself fell into a coma and died the following morning.

Maharani Bamba's grave in Elveden church, *c.* 1890. The royal physician, Dr William Gull, wrote to the Queen, stating that 'Bamba had been in delicate health from diabetes and lately her daughter's illness'.[19] The India Office arranged for her funeral. She was borne by a special train to Thetford station, carried to the graveyard of St Andrew's church on the Elveden estate on 23 September 1887, and was laid to rest in an emotional ceremony, attended by her young children. The Maharajah was absent. The value of her personal estate at death was the paltry sum of £2,001 15*s* 7*d*.

Maharajah Duleep singh, c. 1885. In July 1887 the Maharajah rented a *dacha* in Petro Park, north-west Moscow, but disaster struck a couple of weeks later, triggering a series of mishaps for the aggrieved Maharajah that would leave him ruined. First, on 1 August, Katkov, his only hope of an audience with the Tsar, died. Then came news of the mysterious death of his 'prime minister in exile' Thakur Singh Sandhawalia. (The Maharajah strongly believed his cousin was murdered.) And, finally, he learned that his wife Maharani Bamba had died on 18 September 1887. The broken Maharajah and the heavily pregnant Ada spent the remainder of the year in a boarding house, Hotel Billo, in Bolshoi Lubyanka, Moscow. On 26 December Ada gave birth out of wedlock to a baby girl, Princess Pauline Alexandrina Duleep Singh. The following month Duleep Singh was refused his eagerly awaited audience with the Tsar. This was the final nail in his coffin. Duleep Singh once again felt a sense of rejection and knew that there was nothing more he could do in Russia. In 1889 he moved back to Paris, and in May of that year he proposed to Ada, as she was expecting their second child. Tevis mentioned to the Foreign Office in Whitehall that 'Duleep Singh was married to this woman according to the forms of the Sikh religion some time ago . . . this marriage has been coming on some time'.[21] The wedding took place at the town hall of the 8th arrondisement in Paris on 21 May 1889. On 25 October a second daughter was born to Ada, Princess Ada Irene Helen Benyl Duleep Singh.

On the morning of 13 July 1890 Duleep Singh suffered a stroke. His left side was paralysed, and he could barely speak or pick up a pen. On 18 July, conceding defeat, he asked Prince Victor to write to Queen Victoria for a pardon. The following year, while she was taking a discreet holiday at Grasse in France, the Queen agreed to an audience. Prince Frederick escorted his father to the Grant Hotel in the Alpes Maritimes, as Prince Victor was in Germany. The meeting was an emotional one: the Maharajah broke down and wept beside the Queen. A royal pardon was granted, to the dismay of her ministers.

Back in England his youngest son Prince Edward became ill with pneumonia, and his own health was rapidly declining. The Maharajah travelled back to England to see his little boy, arriving at Hastings on 21 April, and returning to France on the 24th. A week later he learned that his son Prince Edward had died.

The Maharajah's gravestone in Elveden churchyard. At 9.00 p.m. on the night of 21 October 1893 the Maharajah suffered an apoplectic fit and lingered unconscious until the following evening: the next day he was found dead. Ada, who was in London, was among the first to arrive at the scene with Prince Frederick, followed by Prince Victor. It had been the Maharajah's wish to be buried at his place of death,[22] but the family decided to bring him back to his beloved Elveden beside the graves of his first wife and son, Prince Edward. The undertakers, Mr Reginal Goslins, wrote 'no cause of death' on the certificate and there was no post-mortem. The Queen was informed, while the India Office and Foreign Office in London were relieved: the tension of the last forty-four years since the annexation of the Punjab had at last eased, and the most complicated of Intelligence files at Whitehall had come to a close. The British Empire was once again victorious.

On 26 October 1893 the body of the Maharajah was placed on the 9 o'clock boat train at the Gare St Lazare to catch the midnight Dieppe-Newhaven ferry and then to St Pancras for a special train to Thetford, arriving at noon the next day. The body was laid in the chancel of Elveden church, and the funeral arranged for the next day at 12.30 p.m. Surrounding the coffin was a beautiful array of wreaths and crosses, her Majesty's bearing the simple note 'from Queen Victoria', while the Prince of Wales inscribed 'for auld lang syne, Albert Edward'; and from Ada was a magnificent cross composed of a choice of white exotics upon which was the word 'Ada' in violets. There were wreaths and sympathetic notes from all his friends and workers, including his faithful attendant Aroor Singh, and a mysterious wreath from France.

6

Princes Victor and Albert Edward

Prince Victor Duleep Singh, c. 1905, wearing a cravat and three-piece suit. The signed photograph was published in a hunting magazine, a sport of which the prince was very fond.

Maharajah Duleep Singh had three sons. The eldest, Prince Victor, was born on 10 July 1866, followed by Prince Frederick in 1868, and then, on 20 August 1879 Prince Albert Edward Alexander Duleep Singh the youngest of all the Maharajah's six children with Maharani Bamba, affectionately called 'Edward'.

As a young man Prince Victor Duleep Singh studied at Eton[1] before going up to Cambridge, where he met his first and true love, Lady Anne Blanche Alice of Coventry, his good friend George's sister. Family matters took their toll and Prince Victor, with his younger brothers and sisters, was rushed off to India via Aden. In a confidential memorandum, dated 11 February 1886, W.M. Young, the secretary to the Punjab government, wrote to the Foreign Secretary in India, H.M. Durand, that one of the reasons Duleep Singh was coming to India was to arrange the marriage of his eldest children. Prince Victor felt distraught; he never quite understood his father or his quarrels with the British government. On the P&O ship en route to India, he openly objected to his father's actions, and spoke of him as 'my idiotic father'.[2]

On the journey back to England in 1886, the children settled with their mother, Maharani Bamba, at their London residence in Holland Park. The following year Prince Victor joined the Royal Military Academy, getting a special cadetship. Children of Indian extraction were disqualified by parentage from the Army under the existing rules, but Queen Victoria bent the rules for her godson. Prince Victor scraped through two terms at Sandhurst, and was placed 155th in the merit list. He left Sandhurst the following December and was made a lieutenant in the 1st Dragoon Guards. He was honourable ADC to Halifax, and was promoted to captain in 1894, but his military career was a shambles. His interests lay elsewhere, and he resigned in 1898.

Ivory miniature of Queen Victoria and Prince Albert presented to Prince Victor Duleep Singh dated 1867. Prince Victor was christened 'Victor Albert Jay Duleep Singh' at Elveden in 1866. Eight and a half months after his birth the Queen, being the new Prince's godparent, desired a second christening in the private chapel at Windsor Castle. She gave the young prince a framed miniature of herself and Prince Albert, inscribed on the back 'To the Shahazadah Victor Albert from his Godmother Victoria R'.

A carte-de-visite photograph by H. Lenthall of Prince Victor Duleep Singh as a toddler in 1867, wearing Indian dress.

Prince Victor Duleep Singh, *c.* 1871. As a child Prince Victor's hair was kept uncut as was Prince Frederick's, as it was the Maharani's wish that both Princes would retain their long hair until they were twelve years old.[3] Prince Victor was privately educated at Elveden and at their London residence in Kensington, where he and Prince Frederick were tutored by the Revd Arthur Osborne Jay. At an early age the Maharajah would take his sons to shooting parties and Prince Victor in particular became a good marksman like his father. An Elveden gamekeeper recalled 'I remember the Maharajah and his two sons Prince Victor and Prince Frederick having a day in Eriswell, the three of them killing over 600 partridges. I was driving the cartridge cart at the time and 1,700 cartridges were brought out and for the last drive, the stock, now running low was equally divided.'[4]

Prince Victor Duleep Singh, *c.* 1878. The Maharajah's gamekeeper recalled, 'The Princes were both amazingly quick shots, although Victor was rated amongst the very highest, I would not place them in top class for style and grace alone, their build did not assist them in this. All the same, from the killing point of view they needed a lot of beating . . . Cooksey Hill on High Lodge was another good sporting ground, I once saw Prince Victor there in a pit, and the birds were coming over high and fast. He killed two pheasants with his first gun and had three birds falling before the first one hit the ground.'[5] In the 1890's Prince Victor and Frederick would often hire the Weeting Hall estate for shooting; the bag for one season was around 6,000 head, mainly of pheasants and

Princess Catherine, seated on the left, with Prince Albert Edward and Princess Sophia seated on the right, at a fancy dress party, *c.* 1887. After his mother's death, Prince Edward and his sisters moved to 21 Clifton Street, Folkestone, into the care of Mr and Mrs Arthur Oliphant, whose father had been the Maharajah's equerry at Elveden. Prince Edward became very lonely; his father had deserted him at a tender age and his mother had passed away. It seemed almost too much for a boy of his age. He had been brought up as a king's son, surrounded by servants and the plush open spaces at Elveden. His memorable times at Elveden were not to be forgotten, when he played merrily with his younger sister Princess Sophia on their ponies or, after being dressed and groomed, was sent off to extravagant parties with the children of his father's fellow socialites.

Christmas 1891 SANDROYD.

Name	Place at Beginning of Term.	Final Place.	Improvement.	Conduct.
E. Duleep Singh	11	2	G.	Good

Form.	Report in Different Subjects.	Place by Term's Marks.	Number of Boys in Form.	G: Good. F: Fair. B: Bad.	Age.	Average Age of Boys in Form.
III	Classics. Latin.	1	11	Good	12.3	11.8
III	Greek.	5	9	Though rather backward in this subject, he has made good progress lately		
IV	Mathematics.	3	9	His place in this form is very creditable to him F.A.		12½
IV	French.	5	9	Fair		12.6
III	History and Modern Subjects.	1	11	G		11.8
III	Divinity.	1	11	G.		

Form-Master's General Report. Very satisfactory in all his subjects – has worked consistently well, & is a most satisfactory pupil G. H. Bodker

Warden's Report. As shown by the average age of boys in iii Form, he is backward in all subjects except mathematics – he is a hard worker & a most excellent boy L.H.W.W.

The School will reopen Thursday 28th Jan 1892 The train leaves Waterloo at 4.20 Arrives ... at ...

Prince Albert Edward's school report. The Prince was a bright child and the Oliphants sent him to Sandroyd, a private school in Sussex. His form master remarked, 'Edward has worked consistently well, he is a most satisfactory pupil', while his school report for Christmas 1891 showed the young Prince achieving top marks in his form in Latin, Greek, history and modern studies, and divinity. In mathematics he was third, and his warden concluded 'he is a hard worker and a most excellent boy'.[7] A few weeks after this report the Prince contracted pneumonia. Although he later made some improvement, the doctors said there was no chance of his going to Eton and by late April his condition became worse, with tubercular swellings in his stomach. At this time his brothers had gone over to France to visit the equally ill Maharajah, who had suffered a heart attack.

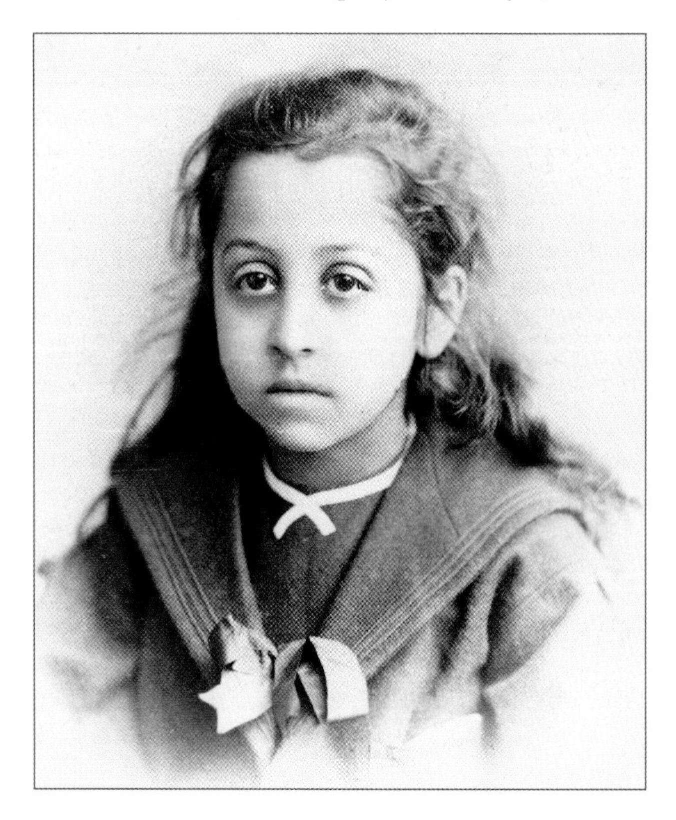

Prince Albert Edward photographed in the studios of Lambert Weston & Son in Folkestone, *c.* 1888. On 21 April 1893 Prince Victor brought the Maharajah back from Paris to see the fragile little Prince Edward. The Maharajah made his emotional trip back to the shores of England and spent the weekend at a hotel in Hastings. Overjoyed to see his little boy, the Maharajah was urged by Prince Victor not to cry or weep bitterly, for fear of distressing the young Prince Edward yet further. Before leaving he gave Prince Edward a piece of paper on which he wrote 'The Lord is my shepherd'. He kissed his little son and returned to Paris on the 24 April. A week later Prince Edward died. He was only thirteen years old.

Prince Victor Duleep Singh in princely attire, *c.* 1896. Prince Victor had 'an olive complexion not darker than an Italian', wrote the journalist of the *Worcester Herald*. He was not exceptionally tall in height, but, on the contrary, rather stout. Taking advantage of his new-found freedom and independence, and his convenient residence in London's Holland Park, Prince Victor was exposed to the haunts of London's fleshpots, becoming a regular visitor to the capital's gambling houses.

Prince Victor Duleep Singh, *c.* 1905. Taking an apartment at 120 Mount Street, Mayfair, Prince Victor entertained friends with high-stake card games. He soon fell into debt, owing £120 to the Duke of Newcastle and £60 to Marcus Milner esq., and in total he owed a staggering £17,721, of which £7,277 was due to bookmakers and money lenders including debts with 'Messrs Goodson, Fry & O'Conor', bookmakers to the gentry. The government stepped in and cleared his debts, which were to be taken out of his allotted pension. General Tevis, the British agent planted on Duleep Singh, had earlier described the Prince as 'a fool living for amusement'. Even through his father's illness and stroke he was amusing himself with his stepmother Ada at Monte Carlo where they both 'played heavily'.[8]

Lady Anne Blanche Coventry, *c.* 1898. Lady Anne Blanche was the youngest daughter of the 9th Earl of Coventry, whose family seat was at Croome Court. She was born on 27 January 1874 and was well known in Worcestershire society as an enthusiastic follower of the hounds and a keen horsewoman. Prince Victor, however, preferred shooting. In October 1889, Prince Victor fell in love with an American lady, Miss J. Turnure, daughter of a banker, but in 1890 he was finally declared bankrupt, and the short engagement was broken off. He immediately rekindled his affection for Lady Anne, whom he had known since his days at Cambridge.

Opposite: Princess Anne Duleep Singh, wearing the Duleep Singh family jewels, once worn by Maharani Jind Kaur, *c.* 1898. On 4 April 1898, at St Peter's in London's Eaton Square, where so many fashionable weddings of the day took place, Lady Anne married Prince Victor. It was a lavish affair, and invitations were sent out to every family of note at that time including Lords Iveagh, Buxton, Rothschild, de Grey, Carnarvon and Albemarle. Long before the ceremony, sightseers and those interested in the Coventry family and that of Prince Victor besieged the church. 'As the strains from the organ gave notice of the bride's arrival, Prince Victor, with his brother Prince Frederick acting as best man, and accompanied by the choir, went in procession up the aisle to meet her.'[9] Princess Bamba and Princess Sophia were among the six chosen bridesmaids, wearing matching dresses with different coloured rosettes. The reception was held at Lord Coventry's town residence in Balfour Place. 'The food was served in the dining room and the cake was cut by the Princess [as Lady Anne was known after her marriage] Victor at the time-honoured precedent. The newly weds left soon after four o'clock to head for Folkestone for their honeymoon, this of course, the signal for the guests departure,'[10] noted the local press. The newly wed couple embarked on a cruise to the East for their honeymoon, with the intention of visiting India. They got as far as Colombo but were prevented from entering India. Soon afterwards Queen Victoria ordered Lady Anne to Court, where she delivered one of her most distressing and chilling of orders: the Princess must vow never to have children and and to live abroad with the Prince. Princess Anne followed the command faithfully to her death.

Prince Victor Duleep Singh and Princess Anne Duleep Singh, *c.* 1910. In 1904 Gertrude Bell, the famous traveller and writer, gave two accounts of meeting the Prince and Princess on a leisure cruise. 'I see Prince Dhuleep [*sic*] Singh and his wife lunching here so I imagine they are fellow travellers. He's an awful little man – I wonder how she could have married him.'[11] But her views changed on being further acquainted with the couple on the same cruise the following year. On landing at Gibraltar at Christmas 1905, she wrote, 'We had plenty of people to play bridge with, my friends Prince and Princess Victor Dhuleep [*sic*] Singh among them. I travelled with them on the same ship last year and they are remarkably good bridge players. She is an Englishwoman and he a Mahratta (I think) but more English than the English and though his appearance is strange he is rather a good sort really – if you do not happen to be his creditor.'[12]

A shooting party at Hockwold Hall, an elegant country house north of Elveden, in October 1898. Standing from left to right are Princess Sophia Duleep Singh, Prince Victor's brother-in-law Viscount Deerhurst, and fourth from the left is Prince Victor Duleep Singh. Seated on the left is Lady Deerhurst with Princess Anne Duleep Singh seated third from the left. Sitting on the ground on the right is Prince Frederick Duleep Singh. When Prince Victor and his new bride took up residence at Hockwold it became obvious that the marriage was not approved of.[13] The happy but odd couple later moved away and settled in Paris, where Prince Victor kept a low profile, making only seasonal visits to his brother at Old Buckenham Hall and later to Blo Norton.[14] During the First World War he was ordered to remain in Paris, but he died on 7 June 1918, without issue. He was buried on 11 June at the Cimetière de Monaco, high up on the hills above Monte Carlo, and special services were carried out at St Martin-in-the-Fields, at Eton, and Trinity College, Cambridge on 26 June 1918.

7

Prince Frederick

A carte-de-visite photograph of Prince Frederick Duleep Singh by J.W. Clarke, at Bury St Edmunds, c. 1876.

Prince Frederick was born on 23 January 1868 at Rutland Gate, Knightsbridge. He was baptised at Elveden church on 2 May 1868 as Frederick Victor Jay Duleep Singh, being named after the German crown prince, later Emperor Frederick. On his return from that exhausting journey to India (undertaken at his father's request), Prince Frederick's first task was to complete his education, going first to Eton and then to Magdalene College, Cambridge, where in 1890 he gained a master's degree in history. He was allotted an allowance of £2,000 from the India Office, so that he could live comfortably – but not so extravagantly as his father. In 1897 he purchased Old Buckenham Hall, a Georgian country house, and by 1906 he was house hunting again, putting the estate on the market with the auctioneers Messrs Lumleys, who advertised it as a 'A Miniature Mansion in a Miniature Park',[1] and claimed that 'for its size the property affords some really excellent shooting and adjoins some of the best shootings in the county, and a large extent of sporting adjoining may be hired'.

After the sale of this property Prince Frederick rented Breckles Cottage, which he renamed Breckles House, in the tiny Norfolk village of Breckles, north of Thetford. Only in 1909 did the Prince finally find the home of his dreams, the sixteenth-century moated Blo Norton Hall, off the main road from Thetford to Diss. His love for this site inspired him to write a lengthy article in the *Norfolk & Norwich Archaeological Society Journal*.[2] He built a chapel at the end of the attic wing and furnished it with old benches, hangings and other suitable ornaments, placing ancient stained glass in its windows and had it dedicated 'to the blessed martyr, King Charles the first'.

As well as being a keen collector of old books, china, glass, stained glass, deeds and coins,[3] the Prince was an enthusiastic archaeologist and historian. As an ardent Jacobite, he had many relics of Stuart interest, including a nightshirt and nightcap of King Charles I. He kept a pendant containing a piece of the block on which Charles I was executed and a locket with a ringlet of his hair among his collection.[4] Visitors to the dining-room at Breckles House, and later in the drawing-room at Blo Norton, recalled a portrait of Oliver Cromwell hanging upside down.[5] He would drive up and down the country with his friend Cleer Alger, the famous photographer. Alger was the agent for Wolsey cars, so transport was not a problem. Together they would visit auction houses and stately homes, purchasing portraits of old noblemen and works by local artists.[6] The prince began compiling a catalogue of the portrait collections in Norfolk, which was published posthumously in 1928 by his friend Edmund Farrer, entitled *Portraits in Norfolk Houses*.

Prince Frederick belonged to many historical societies and organisations, but was most associated with the Norfolk & Norwich Archaeological Society. On 4 February 1897 he was elected member of the Society, paying his year's subscription of 7*s* 6*d*. On 27 May 1903 he was elected vice-president, a post that he held also in 1905 and 1909, and finally became the president in 1924, being re-elected in June 1926.[7] He wrote articles for the *Burlington Magazine*[8] and *Connoisseur*,[9] and another seven Norfolk publications. Interested in all things East Anglian, he served on many committees. He was also vice-president for the Suffolk Institute of Archaeology and Natural History, Fellow of the Society of Arts, Royal Norfolk Agricultural Association and Norfolk Archaeological Trust. He was one of the founders of the Pre-Historic Society of East Anglia, president of the London Society of East Anglians, and a committee member of the Society for the Protection of Ancient Buildings, including the local Advisory Committee for the Protection of Churches. The prince also put his name to the newly formed Operatic Society in 1925 as a vice-president, and was governor of the Thetford Grammar School. Socially he was a member of London's exclusive Whites and Carlton clubs, and was a Fellow of the Society of Antiquaries (FSA).

While in the country, Prince Frederick would visit local parishes and churches, strongly urging them to preserve their buildings. He was wholly against the closure of places of worship, and encouraged the restoration of many neglected churches, such as the old church at Thompson where he was largely responsible for persuading the bishop of Norwich against its closure. He saved Bury Town Hall, a fine example of Adam architecture, from destruction, and took a generous interest in the repairs of the churches at Wymondham and Bradley – these being just some of the many buildings he saved. Prince Frederick was a good churchman, and a rather obstinate Protestant who disliked discussions on religion. He was a great lover of music, with a charming tenor voice. In dressing gown and slippers he would walk about his garden long before his guests were up and then proceed upstairs to the drawing-room to play the piano and sing to himself, while in the evening he would slip away and play soft music. The local folk affectionately called him 'Prince Freddy' and on occasions he inherited his father's name tag of 'the Black Prince'. His generosity was second to none; as one villager recalled, 'Prince Frederick was a charming man, I had the pleasure of speaking to him on many occasions, he was a frequent visitor to my aunt's shop on 144 Victoria Road in Diss. The reason for his visit was because my cousin was in a spinal chair, the prince was very kind and interested in him, in fact he made the arrangements for him to go to the orthopaedic hospital for which he paid the expenses.'[10] As his old friend Walter Rye quoted, 'He was never happier than when helping others.'[11]

Prince Frederick in studio pose taken by J.W. Clarke of Bury St Edmunds, *c.* 1880. the Prince is holding a ceremonial Sikh flywhisk, used for stroking the Holy Scriptures when reciting prayers. Both Prince Frederick and his elder brother Prince Victor were photographed at Clarke's studios in Bury St Edmunds in a series of family photos, of which several duplicate albums were made, one set for each member of the family.

The young Prince Frederick during his college years, *c.* 1884. In their early years, Prince Frederick and Prince Victor were educated privately at Elveden and at their London residence in Kensington. Prince Frederick became very interested in history and archaeology at an early age, spending many hours with his mother and brother in picture galleries and exhibitions. His love for the medieval was inherited from his mother. At Cambridge he maintained this interest and added a good liking for pedigrees and genealogy, showing his genius for collecting things of great value with his very small means, and also belonged to the True Blue Club, which enabled him to indulge in his love of the picturesque dress of the eighteenth century, shorn, alas, of its surroundings.

Prince Frederick in theatrical attire, *c*. 1888. The Prince enjoyed acting, and starred in many local stage acts and pantomimes. Here he is during his college days dressed as the Emperor Julius Caesar. Taking up acting professionally may not have been approved of, but he did continue acting as a hobby throughout his life, performing for example in Arthur Wood's *Bilious Attack* at Didlington on 29 January 1897. The Queen asked the Prince's tutor, the Revd Osborne Jay, what the Prince wished to do as to his future. The Reverend replied that 'the Prince would like to go to the College of Arms'. With no precedent for a prince occupying such a position, the matter was dropped.

Prince Frederick with his horse Jumba at Elveden Hall, with a Mr Williams standing at the entrance, *c*. 1883. During his school years, when spending his holidays at Elveden, Prince Frederick would go for long rides by himself to look at churches and houses, coming back with glowing accounts of the interesting and beautiful things he had seen and the stories and legends connected with them. In his copy books were rough drawings of a pew-head, a church window, and other architectural details, showing whither his thoughts would wander, and sketches of churches and houses that took his fancy.[12]

An elegant sketch of Prince Frederick, drawn by Jerra Collé in Monte Carlo, 1892.

Princesses Catherine and Sophia, with Prince Frederick, *c.* 1900. It is very unusual to see Prince Frederick photographed with his sisters, but his bond with them is evident as wherever he chose to live he made sure they resided near him. Together they would often visit Lady Login, at Gracedieu in Wateringbury, who sympathised with the children as she had done with the Maharajah, expressing concern for the Prince's allowance and profession. She even took pains to purchase a portrait of Maharajah Duleep Singh, sold at auction on the death of the widow of the painter John Partridge.[13] 'I had secured at a few hours notice the painting as the Maharajah's children had no means at the moment at their disposal,' wrote Lady Login, and asked the India Office if they could reimburse her from the Maharajah's stipend, which they were not paying him. The India Office refused.[14]

Prince Frederick dressed as an Indian Prince in 1903. Both he and his brother Prince Victor posed in Indian dress complete with turban and jewels. This popular photograph was published in a chapter on Indian Princes in the 1903 edition of *Munsey's Magazine*. Prince Victor was painted in oils in similar dress by the artist S. Hall in 1879, with a sword in one hand, a matchlock in the other, and loose uncut hair flowing behind.[15]

Prince Frederick Duleep Singh photographed by J.W. Clarke of Bury St Edmunds in 1895. In stature the Prince was a little shorter than the Maharajah, but he oozed the grace of the landed gentry and commanded respect. He always wore his trademark moustache, often fashionably rolled at the ends. Prince Frederick, now a dashing and intellectual young man, wanted to prove his prowess in the Army – after all it was in his blood as previous generations had already proved themselves in warfare. The Prince wanted to be no different.

Prince Frederick with officers of the Loyal Suffolk Hussars at Colchester in 1898. Standing left to right are Captain Hon D. Trollemache, Captain Raymond, Surgeon Lieutenant Martin, Prince Frederick Duleep Singh, Miss Lucas, Captain Whitaker, Lieutenant Hon J. Petre, Lieutenant E. Crawley, F. Jarvis and Major Colvin. Seated from left to right are Mrs Wren, Miss Lucas, Lady Gwendoline Colvin, Colonel A.G. Lucas, Mrs A. Lucas, Lieutenant Colonel Cruickshank and Major Baird.

Prince Frederick in the uniform of the Loyal Suffolk Hussars, *c.* 1895. The Prince enrolled in the Loyal Suffolk Hussars (Suffolk Yeomanry) in the regiment's centenary year, and was appointed second lieutenant on 12 August 1893. He was promoted to captain in 1898 and was admitted a Member of the Royal Victorian Order (MVO) in 1901, which was designed for recognition of personal services to Queen Victoria. In the same year he transferred to the King's Own Royal Regiment Norfolk Imperial Yeomanry, and was promoted to the rank of major.

Prince Frederick stands at ease in his Norfolk Yeomanry uniform at Bury St Edmunds in 1897. The Prince was the most photographed member of his family, but his smile for this military photograph taken by Lieutenant E.M. Lucas is quite rare.

Prince Frederick in the Loyal Suffolk Hussars, with officers at Bury St Edmunds in 1901. Standing left to right are Lieutenant B. Hope, Lieutenant W.H. Heal, Mr G.D. Norman and Major W.R. Greene. Seated from left to right are Major H.P. Levita, Lieutenant G.S. Whitfield, Major E.W.D. Baird, Lieutenant Colonel Cruickshank, Lieutenant G. Strutt and Lieutenant Prince Frederick Duleep Singh.

Prince Frederick on horseback in 1915. The Prince resigned his commission in 1908, but re-joined as a major in October 1914 on the outbreak of the First World War. He was gazetted to the 2nd/1st Norfolk Yeomanry,[16] serving in France from 1917 to 1919.[17] He spent much time with training units, and in France he was at a rest camp for artillery horses from the front where this photograph was taken. Here he was area commandant and, during the temporary illness of his devoted batman Herbert Hudson, he enjoyed having to clean his own boots and buttons.[18] He did not, however, see active service.

Prince Frederick at camp during the First World War, photographed here by his fellow officer and friend, Captain Wilson from King's Lynn. The Prince is standing beside his tent which even had the Prince's Coat-of-Arms on it.

Prince Frederick with a fellow officer, in 1915.

Prince Frederick is captured here by Captain Wilson's camera during the First World War. The Prince is standing on the far left, with Captain Clifford Wilson of the Norfolk Yeomanry standing third from the left. During his career the Prince was awarded the Coronation Medal in 1902 and 1911, and was appointed to the General Staff in 1918.

Prince Frederick in a bowler hat, 1895. The Prince's style, attitude and manners were described as those of a country squire, a position he became familiar with. He was a well-mannered man, whose pleasantries were well known. On one occasion, when walking his dog in the village, he went out of his way to go to the back door of a villager's house to apologise for his dog having disturbed a broody hen.

Prince Frederick on horseback, 1914. The Prince is on the left, with Lt Col Seymour and Col Morse with the King's Own Royal Regiment Norfolk Imperial Yeomanry in 1914.

Prince Frederick's first house, Old Buckenham Hall, 1897. The Prince's head gardener John Edwards can be seen here standing second from the left behind a lawnmower, outside the Hall. John Edwards's wife Anne was also in the service of Prince Frederick as a cook. The 340-acre estate enjoyed a well-timbered park, commodious stabling, gardens with pleasure grounds and shrubberies. It also included four farms with homesteads, cottages and other smallholdings, all of which the Prince tenanted. He had a small sporting ground, and often hired adjoining shootings for his personal use. It was his custom to hold an annual dinner party for all the estate tenants and those from whom he hired the shootings. During his time at Old Buckenham, Prince Frederick was mostly occupied with the yeomanry. On his return he would try to lay out the grounds with fine gardens and lawns. He also had a cricket ground[19] built to the rear of the Hall. Although he transformed the grounds into a formal garden he showed great dissatisfaction with his efforts: 'Nothing goes right, the garden is a failure . . . it is disgusting . . . peoples borders are gorgeous – mine are in swarms', he wrote in his diary entry for 9 October 1904.[20]

Blo Norton Hall, *c.* 1920. After a three-year spell in Breckles Cottage, Prince Frederick moved in August 1909 to Blo Norton Hall, which he rented from the Goldson family. The landlord's agent was John Gaze of Diss, whose son recalled an amusing episode when visited by the Prince during his tenancy: 'One day our housemaid came to my father and said "There is a black man at the door, said you would know him and I have put him in the breakfast room – I hope that it was alright." My father was not amused.'[21] The gardens at Blo Norton Hall had much more success and flourished. Avenues of clipped beeches were planted. The gardens also had a centrepiece sundial with statuettes placed at either end. A stone figure of Adonis adorned the fish pond and there was another of Atlas, which stood in the centre of the garden.[22]

The Black Prince's Temple, photographed in 1923. Adjoining the Hall is a small woodland where Prince Frederick cleared an avenue of trees from the main road to open up a delightful vista. At the end of the lime avenue, in a pine grove, he built a little white-pillared folly which he dedicated to the 'Divine Winds of Heaven'. It fondly became known as the 'Black Prince's Temple' and it is commonly believed that the Prince built it in memory of his father's religion. Here the Prince would spend his time in the cool summer air, reading and listening to the music of the breezes in the pines, passing his time peacefully.

Prince Frederick at an Elveden gathering in 1911 standing third from the left, with Lord Bristol and Lord Iveagh to his left. In the front row are Lady Iveagh, Miss E. Guinness, Ernest Guinness and Mr Kingsbury. The Prince and his aristocratic friends would often be invited to shooting parties on the renowned estate at Elveden. Prince Frederick still kept up his interest in the sport, which his father had much favoured. He had inherited his father's quick eye on the muzzleloader.

The gallery at Blo Norton Hall, *c.* 1920. On careful examination the photograph shows the Schoefft paintings, *Maharajah Sher Singh* and *Ranjit Singh at the Golden Temple in Amritsar* hanging opposite one another.[30] The Prince also displayed his father's extensive art collection of paintings from the Sikh kingdom, and in the hall hung his extensive portrait collection of Norfolk worthies.

Prince Frederick Duleep Singh, *c.* 1897. A regular member of his local parish in Blo Norton, Prince Frederick would be seen coming down from the Hall on Sundays in his bowler hat, chalk-stripe suit and walking stick for morning service where he would joyfully sing in the choir.[23] He would occasionally read the lesson: 'I can vividly recall him reading the scriptures with his rather clipped voice,' added an old resident.[24] He insisted that his guests go with him to church and join him in singing lustily. On one particular Sunday the organist of the parish asked someone else to deputise for her as she was going on holiday. After the service the rector's wife introduced the deputy organist to the Prince. The Prince then said, 'It is the first time I have been able to sing a certain note, the other good lady always plays a fancy note of her own.' He evidently took his singing seriously and for a special service he would join the choir in the choir stalls.[25]

Prince Frederick posing at a shooting party at Elveden in December 1924. The Prince is standing third from the left, with Captain Dennison, General Inkwell and Lord Iveagh seated at the front. He would regularly visit Elveden, stopping over for tea at the Iveaghs'. His vast correspondence with Lord Iveagh showed how close he remained to his old home's new owner. From his earlier research into the Elveden estate, Prince Frederick supplied Lord Iveagh with much history on the Hall, including the plans of the building works his father had carried out when he moved there in the 1860s. Lord Iveagh wished to extend the Hall to twice its size, and Prince Frederick obliged with all its old property plans, papers and notes.[26]

Prince Frederick can be seen reading peacefully in the garden of Blo Norton Hall, *c.* 1925, with a part of his huge library visible from the outside. The book collection now forms The Prince Duleep Singh Reading Room at Thetford Library. Although a keen cricketer and an avid tennis player, with his own tennis court built during his stay at Breckles House, the Prince's true passions lay in reading and collecting books. His magnificent antiquarian book collection formed one of Norfolk's finest private libraries.

The Ancient House Museum, 1928. Prince Frederick shared his father's affection for the historical town of Thetford and decided it was time it had its own exhibition house. In 1921 the Prince very generously purchased the old Tudor house in White Hart Street, known as the Ancient House, and presented it to the mayor and corporation of Thetford for this purpose.

The opening of the Ancient House Museum, 11 December 1924. The Mayor of Thetford is flanked by the Duchess of Grafton, with Prince Frederick Duleep Singh in his fur coat for this press photograph for the *Eastern Daily Press*. The fifteenth-century house was carefully restored at an estimated cost of £550 and to start the museum Prince Frederick donated many relics and artefacts of local interest from his personal collection.

Prince Frederick Duleep Singh at Blo Norton Hall. In 1926 Prince Frederick fell critically ill. During the previous few months his health had been in decline, but on Thursday 12 August 1926 he suffered a heart attack. His sisters immediately surrounded him and the family received a message of inquiry from the King on the Saturday. Sadly, the much loved last Prince of Lahore passed away at Blo Norton Hall at 2.30 p.m. on Sunday afternoon, 15 August, at the age of fifty-eight. The funeral took place the following Thursday at St Andrew's church in Blo Norton and was conducted by the Rector, the Revd C.L. Norris, assisted by the Revd Osborne Jay of Thornbury.

The funeral of Prince Frederick, 19 August 1926. The wheeled bier was met by the chief mourners, Princesses Bamba, Catherine and Sophia. Princess Pauline was also present, as was Princess Anne Duleep Singh. The grave was in brick, the 400-year-old bricks having been purchased by Prince Frederick some years earlier from an old house. Among those attending were a great many local folk, including representatives and friends of the various societies and organisations with which Prince Frederick was associated, and the Duke of Grafton, Lord Henniker, the Countess of Albemarle and the Mayor of Thetford, with many other landed gentry and officials. Floral tributes came from the parishioners of Blo Norton, the farmers of Blo Norton, the Cricket Club at Blo Norton, Whites Club, the Carlton Club, and comrades past and present of the Norfolk Yeomanry. The Prince was the last male heir of the once illustrious Sikh durbar. Tragically, to keep his peace with the authorities, Prince Frederick never set foot in the Punjab to witness the marvels over which his family's rule had extended. His death put an end to the legacy of the Sikh Kingdom.

8

Princess Catherine

A fine full-face portrait of the beautiful, European-looking Princess Catherine Duleep Singh, c. 1890.

The Maharajah's second daughter, Catherine Hilda Duleep Singh, was born on 27 October 1871. It was while in the care of Mr and Mrs Oliphant at Folkestone that Princess Catherine would meet her governess, Fräulein 'Lina' Schafer, twelve years her senior. The German governess from Kassel would become the Princess's life-long confidante and would change her life for ever. In addition to the governess, violin and singing tutors were also employed, together with a swimming instructor. The following year Lina Schafer took the Princess to the Black Forest, Kassel and Dresden. The odd pair were forming a very special and intimate bond.

In 1903 Princess Catherine embarked on a tour of India, visiting Lahore, Kashmir, Dalhousie, Simla, and the holy Sikh city of Amritsar.[1] Here she recalled meeting Sikh elders at the ongoing Diwali festivities who had fought under her grandfather, Maharajah Ranjit Singh. 'The Diwali festival was yesterday; there were illuminations at the Golden Temple and at the Tank.[2] The fireworks were let off from one side of thc tank, the effect of the reflections in the water were very pretty.'[3] She surprisingly knew much about her ancestral past and took great interest in it: 'I visited the salt range, at Pind Dadun Khan.' [These were the very ones Maharajah Duleep Singh had talked about recovering from the government in 1885, as he claimed they were his personal ancestral property.] 'There remains a strong fortress in a gateway built by Maha [sic] Singh, which was most interesting.'[4] On her passage towards the Khyber Pass, she added, 'Before the gates to the pass is the Fort of Jamrud, where Hari Singh[5] was, and where he died fighting.' In February 1904 she visited the Sikh princely states of Kapurthala, Nabha, Jind and Patiala: 'We met the Rajas in each case except Patiala: but we met the late Maharaja's brother and President at dinner.' She left India at the end of March 1904.

The Princess spent most of her subsequent life in Europe, dividing her time between her family in Switzerland and the company of Lina Schafer in Kassel. But when Lina died on 27 August 1937, at the age of seventy-eight, the Princess felt that Kassel had nothing to offer her. Advised by her neighbour and accountant, Dr Fritz Ratig, she left the country in November 1937. The Princess sold everything and fled, arriving back in England via Switzerland.

Princess Catherine Duleep Singh photographed at six years old, in the studios of J.W. Clarke, Bury St Edmunds, 1877.

The Maharajah's brother-in-law, Wilhelm Alexander Muller (1854–1934). Wilhelm was the eldest of Maharani Bamba's brothers, and was affectionately known as 'Willy'. As a child, Princess Catherine accompanied her mother to Europe on several occasions when she visited her uncle Wilhelm Alexander Muller in Switzerland. Later in life Princess Catherine often visited the other Muller family members in Germany, usually before or after her visit to the Bayreuth Festival. Between 1928 and 1930 she made several trips to Switzerland, visiting her uncle and his son Karl.

Charlotte Maria Muller and Adolf Schmidt. Princess Catherine was also close to her aunt, Charlotte Muller, daughter of Ludwig Muller and half-sister of Maharani Bamba. Charlotte poses here with her husband at Kassel. She sent this photograph to the Princess inscribed, 'With love, Adolf & Charlotte Schmidt, 1889.'

Prince Edward with his sisters, Princesses Catherine, Bamba and Sophia in the late 1880s. In the autumn of 1889 Princess Catherine, together with her sisters, moved from Folkestone to the Oliphants' Brighton House, at No. 5 Sussex Square. In September 1890 Princesses Catherine and Bamba went off to Oxford where at Somerville Hall, under Principal Miss Agnes Catherine Maitland, Princess Catherine passed all her exams.

The three Princesses, *c.* 1892. Princess Catherine was growing up to become the most beautiful of the three sisters; her fair complexion, high cheek bones and slender figure gave her a very European appearance. The Princesses are photographed here at their formal presentation at court, with Princess Catherine standing behind Princess Bamba and Princess Sophia.

Princess Catherine's governess, Lina Schafer, photographed in Kassel, *c.* 1890. The precise nature of the relationship was never known, but the continued spinsterhood of a woman as beautiful as Princess Catherine suggests much. She was not only close to Lina Schafer but also her family. She began attaching herself more to the German family than to her own, although the relationship was never really approved of by the Schafer family.

An invitation for Princess Catherine Duleep Singh to attend the coronation of King George V and Queen Mary at Westminster Abbey in 1911.

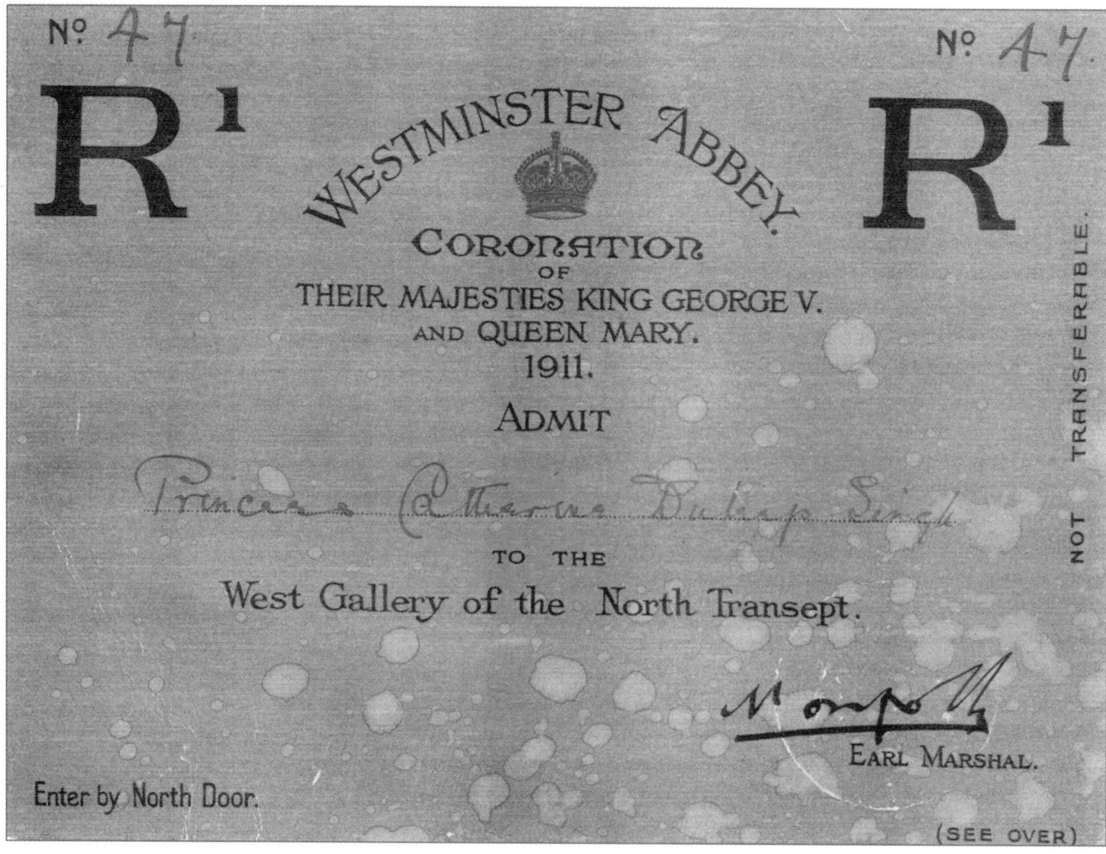

No. 47 No. 47

R1 R1

WESTMINSTER ABBEY.

CORONATION
OF
THEIR MAJESTIES KING GEORGE V.
AND QUEEN MARY.
1911.

ADMIT

Princess Catherine Dulip Singh

TO THE
West Gallery of the North Transept.

EARL MARSHAL.

NOT TRANSFERABLE.

Enter by North Door.

(SEE OVER)

Princess Catherine's old house in Kassel. On the outbreak of the First World War Princess Catherine went to Germany until 1918, returning to Kassel in 1920, where she took up residence at Villa am Mulans. Frau Christina Telker, a neighbour's child, recalled, 'the old Princess would always walk on Fraulein Schafer's left, out of respect for her teacher – who would say, "we are like two little mice living in a little house". The inside of the Villa am Mulang was full of Chippendale furniture and luxurious tapestries. The Princess worked in the garden but never cooked. They would lunch every day in the nearby Pension Blankenburg.'[6]

Princess Catherine's Buckinghamshire home, Coalhatch House, *c.* 1940. On her return from Kassel after Lina Schafer's death, Princess Catherine moved into the six-bedroom Coalhatch House in Penn, while her sister, Princess Sophia, moved across the road into The Rathenrea. The Second World War had broken out and London was a prime bombing target, so Penn was much safer than their residence at Faraday House near Hampton Court Palace. Coalhatch House had its own library and music room, both lined with books and ample grounds with laid-out gardens, including an orchard.

Princess Catherine with Dr and Mrs Haunstein, *c.* 1940. During the war a Jewish family, the Haunsteins, arrived at Coalhatch House. Friends of Princess Catherine, they changed their name to Haughton but the villagers became suspicious. 'The Haunsteins' son George was a clever boy; he went to Cambridge. The daughter Ursula studied English, and they would both be seen riding their bicycles in the village. Their mother loved sewing, and made hats among other things.'[7] There was also a violinist, Samuel Volgarioff, another of Princess Catherine's entourage from Germany, who lived at Coalhatch House. He would sometimes play at dinner, and at the children's parties he would go around playing the violin.

The Princess passed away peacefully on the night of Sunday 8 November 1942 at her home in Penn, aged seventy-one.[8] The cause of death was said to be heart failure.[9] It was her wish to be cremated and on 12 November her beautifully decorated coffin was placed at Coalhatch House so that all her servants and friends could pay their last respects before the cortège was borne from Penn to Golders Green crematorium in north London.[10] The chief mourner and only family member present was Princess Sophia, as Princess Bamba was stranded in India due to the war.

9

Princess Sophia

Maharani Bamba holding Princess Sophia Duleep Singh, c. 1877.

Princess Sophia, the youngest of the Maharajah's three daughters with Maharani Bamba, was born on 8 August 1876. She was christened Sophia Jindan Alexdrowna Duleep Singh, named Sophia after Maharani Bamba's mother and Jinda after Duleep Singh's mother.

It was during Princess Sophia's illness in September 1887 that her mother passed away. The frail Maharani had spent all night praying beside her little girl and fell into a coma herself, dying the following morning. After the death of their mother, Princess Sophia was put under the care of Arthur Oliphant with her sisters and little brother Prince Albert Edward.

In 1906 Prince Frederick rented the lavish Blo Norton Hall, and around the same time he purchased the Thatched Cottage in Blo Norton for his sisters. The sisters conveniently named the cottage Hampton House after Hampton Court Palace, which was located opposite the Princesses' London home, Faraday House. Hampton House was much like a mini palace, having regal, French-style doors, with steps leading up to the garden. As you went down the garden, the path had trellises of roses on either side like an avenue. Inside the house were beautiful Tudor beams, with a large warm fire, a grand piano at which the sisters spent many joyful hours,[1] elegant Mughal screens brought back from their visits to India and a mouth-piece telephone,[2] one of only three in the village.[3]

Princess Sophia joined the Suffragette movement and became a leading figure in the Women's Social and Political Union (WSPU), fighting for the right for women to vote in Britain. On 22 May 1911 Spelthorne Petty Sessions summoned the Princess for keeping a carriage, a manservant and five dogs without licences, and for using armorial bearings. Mr Leon Castello, who appeared for the Princess, said she very much regretted that she could not attend the court herself. He admitted seven of the summonses, except that relating to the armorial bearings. The Princess had asked him to protest on her behalf against the injustice of making women, who had no voice in the management of the country, liable to taxation. The chairman said that they had nothing to do with that, and the Bench decided to fine the Princess £1 for not taking out dog licences, £1 for keeping a non-licensed male servant, and £1 for keeping an unlicensed carriage. The question of keeping an armorial bearing was reserved.[4] She appeared in court again in December 1913, accompanied by fellow members of the league, for keeping two dogs and a carriage without licences. She made a stand stating that 'taxation without representation' was a tyranny. She added, 'I am unable conscientiously to pay money to the State, as I am not allowed to exercise any control over its expenditure, neither am I allowed any voice in the choosing of

Members of Parliament, whose salaries I have to help to pay. This is very unjust. When the women of England are enfranchised and the State acknowledges me as a citizen I shall, of course, pay my share willingly towards its upkeep. If I am not a fit person for the purposes of representation, why should I be a fit person for taxation?'[5]

During the First World War, Princess Sophia organised patriotic flag days for Punjabi troops in the Indian Army. She even went so far as to visit wounded Indian soldiers at Brighton Pavilion where they were being nursed. Many were honoured at meeting the granddaughter of the great Ranjit Singh, and requested mementos to take back home. She obliged, handing out signed photographs of herself. One such soldier of the 15th Sikhs was Kartar Singh, who wrote home to the Punjab from his sick bed at Milford-on-Sea in 1916, 'My friend this is the photo of our king's granddaughter – he who was King of the Sikhs, Ranjit Singh. She has distributed her photo amongst Sikh brethren at the depot [Milford] on the evening of the 23 February at five o'clock.'[6]

Princess Sophia took part in the 10,000-strong 'Women's War Work' procession led by Mrs Emmeline Pankhurst. She joined the Suffragette Fellowship after the First World War, remaining a member to the end of her life. After Mrs Pankhurst's death in 1928, she was appointed president of the committee.[7]

Left: Princess Sophia and her younger brother Prince Edward at Folkestone in 1887. The little innocent-looking princess was very attached to Prince Albert Edward. They would play hand in hand, sharing the same playmates, and enjoying the freedom of the open grounds of Elveden Hall. She enjoyed private tuition in her early days at Elveden before hurriedly being packed off with her siblings on their painstaking journey to India via Aden. Too young to understand the inner details and particulars of the move, she would have enjoyed the cruise on the SS *Verona* like any other unsuspecting child of her age.

Below left: Princess Sophia photographed at a studio, c. 1892.

Opposite above: A Lafayette photograph of Princess Catherine and Princess Sophia Duleep Singh dressed in saris with beautiful Indian jewellery, *c.* 1895.

Opposite below: Princess Sophia with her American Columbia bicycle. The photograph was published by *The Sketch* in 1896, which wrote 'Both Princess Sophia and Princess Bamba are very fond of the outdoor life and simple amusement which are felt to be in England the birthright of every happy, healthy girl, be she Princess or peasant. They are both as fond of sport and of animals as are the Prince and Princess Victor Duleep Singh, and Princess Sophia is not only a first-rate cyclist, but she has long been a devoted adherent of the Ladies Kennel Association, often showing her pets at the L.K.A. Shows.'

Faraday House, opposite Hampton Court Palace, *c.* 1920. Princess Sophia was given this grand, three-storey house in 1896 as a grace and favour home by Queen Victoria. In 1897 the Manor House was also rented, being ideally situated near Old Buckenham Hall, occupied by her brother Prince Frederick. Princess Sophia would wake at dawn and take her three dogs for their morning walk in the gardens of Hampton Court Palace, for which she had her own personal set of keys.

Princess Sophia as a guest of the American industrialist, Bradley Martin, at the Balmacaan Estate, 11 September 1898. Bradley Martin was a tenant at the beautiful sixteenth-century Balmacaan Estate in Scotland, and a benefactor to the local community. Seated from left to right are Colonel Larking, Princess Sophia Duleep Singh, the Countess of Silkirk, Lady Helen Craven, Mrs Bradley Martin, Lady Beatrice Kaye and the Honourable Walter Catchpole. Mr Bradley Martin stands to the far right wearing a hat, while his son Martin stands directly behind the Countess of Silkirk.

Princess Sophia's nephew, Pritam Singh Sandhawalia, at a United Indian Association gathering, seated front centre, *c.* 1920. In 1907 Princess Sophia took charge of her nephew, son of her cousin Gurdit Singh Sandhawalia, supporting him financially and paying for his education in India. Since Thakur Singh Sandhawalia's involvement with Maharajah Duleep Singh in the 1880s the family had formed a close bond, and the Princesses kept in regular contact. Princess Sophia looked upon Pritam Singh as her son.

Princess Sophia's cousin Sardar Gurdit Singh Sandhawalia. The Princess wrote to Gurdit Singh, 'I will be more than happy to have either of your sons, ideally the youngest one of ten years, with me in England, to be educated. I cannot speak Urdu or Punjabi, so he will need to learn to speak English.'[8] She did not offer to pay his travelling expenses, so the trip to England never materialised. She added, 'of course you realise that having anything to do with us, will not gain him any high posts in India, in fact it will probably do the opposite thing, as the government are not fond of us'. This suggests that the Foreign Office was still interfering in their lives. She sent Pritam Singh £18 half yearly in January and July, and was regularly kept informed of his progress.

Princess Sophia selling *The Suffragette* outside Hampton Court Palace in 1913. The strongest-willed of the three sisters, Princess Sophia would often be seen selling this WSPU paper and attend demonstrations. An active member from 1909 to 1914, her yearly subscription ranged from £6 to £30 annually, quite a considerable sum for that time. In addition, she was a member of the Women's Tax Resistance League (WTRL), whose main objective was the refusal to pay taxes of various kinds.[9] Her sister Princess Catherine also joined the movement as a member of the National Union of Women's Suffrage Societies (NUWSS), but did not get actively involved in demonstrations.

Princes Sophia delivering *The Suffragette* by horse and cart around London's theatres and matinée houses, seated on the right in the front carriage, *c.* 1910. Princess Sophia also donated to the cause, including gifts for the WSPU Christmas bazaar in 1911. She was one of the notable representatives present with Mrs Pankhurst at Caxton Hall on 18 November 1910, known as 'Black Friday', when the Suffragettes went to the House of Commons to see the prime minister. Uniformed and plain clothed police were among the crowd, and on the orders of the Home Secretary, women were thrown from one to the other. In consequence of these instructions many of the women were severely hurt and several were knocked down and bruised.[10]

Princess Sophia standing in the garden of Faraday House, Hampton Court, *c.* 1920. Although the Princess had been given this grace and favour home in 1896, it was not until ten years later that she actually moved in, after leaving the Manor House in Old Buckenham.

Princess Sophia with her godchild Catherine Alexdrowna Lane, *c.* 1940. Catherine Alexdrowna was the daughter of Princess Sophia's personal maid and chauffeur, Ivy and John Lane, who gave the Princess many years of faithful service: their child took the Princess's middle name of Alexdrowna. After Prince Frederick's death in 1926, Blo Norton Hall continued to be occupied by the Princesses until the lease ran out in 1935. She told her nephew Pritam Singh, 'I and my two sisters have been in Norfolk for about two months shifting up a house that belonged to my brother, which we kept on for nine years, it has been a great task dividing the furniture, pictures, etc but is completed at last.'[11] The task of cataloguing the items and making an inventory was given to her loyal maid, Miss Ivy, and John Lane.

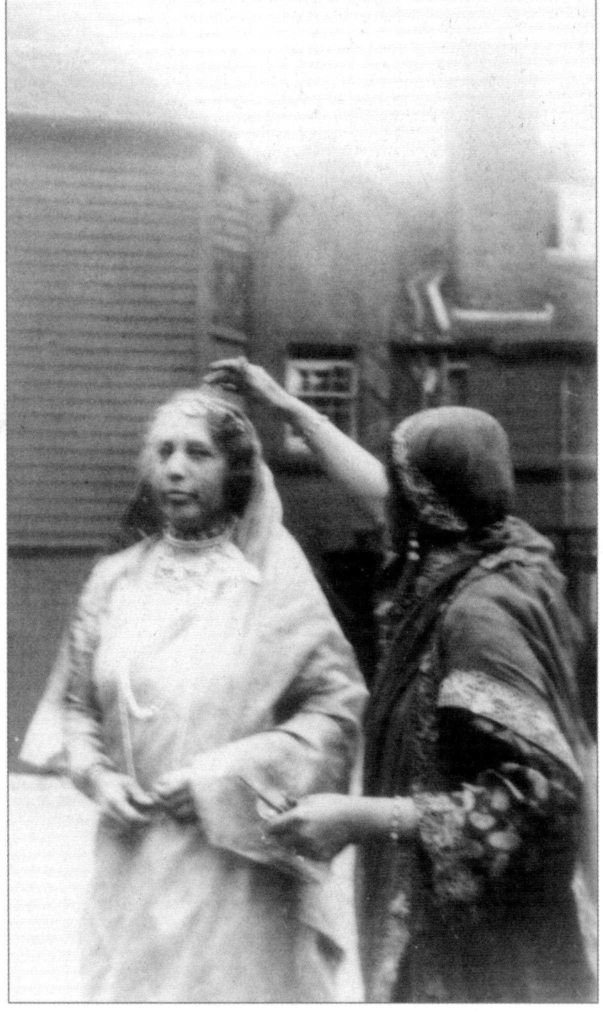

Princess Sophia being dressed in a sari by an Indian lady, probably taken at a Punjab Hill station. In 1907 and in 1924 Princess Sophia visited India with Princess Bamba, touring Kashmir, Lahore, Amritsar and Murree. The first trip was a quiet one to Lahore, but the second one attracted too much attention. The sisters entered Lahore amid a noisy crowd, who had come to see the daughters of their last king. They were dressed in their finery, one in a bottle-green and the other in a maroon sari, in fine French georgette, a kind of chiffon, fringed with gold and precious stones. Wearing exquisite traditional *kundan* jewels – long earrings of pure gold faced with enamel-encrusted diamonds – they caused quite a scene and the authorities were displeased. The police dispersed the crowd, as it was politically far too dangerous.[12] From Lahore Princess Sophia stopped off at Amritsar with Princess Bamba and her husband Colonel Sutherland. She proceeded with her brother-in-law to Kashmir on 27 March 1924, where she stayed for six weeks from mid-April. 'There has been a great deal of rain, but it is a beautiful country, and I am very glad to be here,' she told her nephew Pritam Singh.[13]

Princess Sophia with Sardar Bahadur Mohan Singh, *c.* 1937. Mohan Singh was a member of the Council of the Secretary of State for India in London between 1935 and 1940,[14] and is pictured here wearing a turban standing with his wife, Lajvanti, behind Princess Sophia. Besides her fight for women's emancipation in Britain, Princess Sophia took a great interest in India's political situation, telling her cousin in India, 'I do hope that the "Round Table Conference" will do something to settle the conflicting questions'.[15] The Princess' links with her countrymen remained strong; she supported the native Indian seamen and sailors who were often stranded in London, as evidenced by her subscription to the Lascars Club.

Princesses Sophia and Catherine at an annual Suffragette dinner on 13 October 1938. After the final victory of the Suffragette movement Princess Sophia kept in touch with fellow ex-Suffragettes.

Evacuee Michael Sarbutt standing outside Rathenrae House, 1940. The window to the right was Princess Sophia's bedroom. On the outbreak of the Second World War the Princesses took homes away from the Blitz in London and Buckinghamshire. The quiet village of Penn seemed appropriate, as it was close enough to London and its amenities, and convenient for Blo Norton. Princesses Sophia and Catherine both moved to Hammersley Lane in Penn. Princess Catherine resided in the elegant country home, Coalhatch House,[16] while Princess Sophia chose Rathenrea, a bungalow situated across the road.[17] Although Princess Sophia had her privacy and her beloved dogs at Rathenrea, which Princess Catherine detested, the sisters still spent most of the day together at Coalhatch House. Much to the dislike of Princess Catherine, Princess Sophia was also a heavy smoker – her favourite brand of Cassingbrown was delivered to her in bulk with her weekly supplies from the Army & Navy Stores in London. The young evacuee Michael Sarbutt saw this as an open invitation, and would pinch some cigarettes to smoke behind the sheds. But the Princess was too clever: 'Where's that little Pickle?' (her affectionate name for little Michael). 'I think he has been smoking my cigarettes, because I have a hundred in a box and that lasts me three days, and it's lasted me two and a half days, he must have been at my cigarettes.'[18]

Opposite: Princess Sophia with her pet parrot Akbar during the Second World War, photographed by evacuee John Sarbutt. Shirley Sarbutt remembered the time well: 'The Princess was such a pleasant and kind lady. Here I was living in a most splendid house. On our birthday Princess Sophia would lay a big spread and we was allowed to invite our friends from the school. I was at Penn between 1939 and 1943, where we had ample food and surrounded by oriental ornaments and a talking parrot by the name of "Akbar". The princess had two parrots kept in cages, which she had brought back from India. My brothers would joyfully play with the parrots and the three dogs the princess kept. I remember the night "Akbar" died, Princess Sophia really died with it, as she had much affection for her feathered pet. The other white bird lived for many years.' The evacuee added, 'Princess Sophia had a large air raid shelter built in the grounds, on the nightly raids we would be in the shelter with Princess Sophia and of course her three dogs, she would not leave the dogs. Princess Catherine would not be there obviously because of them.'[19]

Standing from left to right are Shirley Sarbutt, Mrs Sarbutt holding little Catherine Alexdrowna and local girl Beryl, in the orchard of Rathenrae. Like many country folk during the war, Princess Sophia took in evacuee children, John, Michael and Shirley Sarbutt, two brothers and a sister from west London. The Princesses had requested that they would take three children if they were from the same family and had someone there with them. The Sarbutts were chosen because their mother was a teacher, and could be with them. Similarly, two evacuees were taken in at Hampton House in Blo Norton, Albert Hull and William Meadows, both from Hackney, who were taken care of by the house's head maid Dora Crowe.

One of the last photographs of Princess Sophia, in the garden of Rathenrae. In her old age Princess Sophia would wake up at midday, eat her evening meal late at night between 9 p.m. and 10 p.m., and go to bed at about 2 a.m.[20] On 22 August 1948 she died in her sleep. Her solicitor, Henry Charles Wanstall of Chancery Lane, arranged for the cremation at Golders Green on 26 August.[21] It was her request that a full band should play Wagner's *Funeral March* at her cremation, and that her ashes be taken to India for burial.[22]

10

Princess Bamba

Princess Bamba Duleep Singh, c. *1870.*
A carte-de-visite photograph of Princess Bamba as a baby.

Princess Bamba was born in London on 29 September 1869, a year after her brother Prince Frederick. She was baptised Bamba Sofia Jindan Duleep Singh, named after her mother and grandmothers respectively.

Her only known courtship was that with Lieutenant-Colonel David Waters Sutherland,[1] a doctor in the Indian Army who became Principal at King Edward's Medical College, Lahore, from 1909 to 1921. The couple married in 1915, when the Princess was aged forty-six.

Princess Bamba frequently visited India during the days of the British Raj, and made several short trips to India, but was forced to settle at Lahore for longer than she had anticipated in January 1941 as she could not get passage back on account of the war. In 1942 the tragic news of Princess Catherine's death arrived. Princess Bamba was stranded; she could not be present at her sister's last rites. It was a terrible shock to her, especially as she had not been well herself for some months.[2] As her stay was to be a long one, she bought a house in Lahore, which she named The Gulzar, at No. 16 Jail Road. She returned to England in September 1946, and a year later India became independent, which resulted in the formation of Pakistan. The Punjab suffered the most with the border between the two nations split right down the middle of the territory. Princess Bamba's beloved Punjab and the kingdom of her forefathers ceased to exist.

After her husband's death some years earlier, and her sister Princess Sophia's death in 1948, Princess Bamba became very lonely. Her health began to fail further after the death of her younger sister, but she kept herself going by keeping busy and moving from one of her homes to another. She gave up the grace and favour home at Faraday House in Hampton Court[3] and began to share her time between Penn and Blo Norton. She took Princess Sophia's ashes to India for burial in accordance with her sister's last wish. 'A flight is quite easy to obtain but this time I came by land as I brought my darling sister's ashes with me, she did not like flights,'[4] she told Pritam Singh on her arrival. Her next trip was to Kassel, where she arrived unexpectedly in 1949 at the house of Dr Schafer, an unmarried female medical doctor and relation of Fräulein Schafer. A fellow guest of Dr Schafer recalled, 'Bamba arrived from nowhere, bringing in her luggage Princess Catherine's urn, telling us it had been Catherine's last wish to be buried in Kassel.'

Back in England, Princess Bamba began styling herself Queen of the Punjab. She had her father's rebellious nature and seemed the most aggrieved of the siblings.[5] On visiting a high street bookstore in Norwich she once told her driver George Davey to park outside the store, which caused a traffic build-up. A policeman requested, 'Madam, please move the car.' She replied in her stern voice,

'Do you know who you are talking to? I am the Queen of the Punjab.'[6] The grumpy Princess would dress in her finery when visited at Blo Norton by her Sikh countrymen, who had started migrating in the early 1900s, and enjoy all the attention she could get.[7] During this period she was also visited at Hilden Hall by her cousin Karl Wilhelm Muller, grandson of Ludwig Muller, by which time she was already dreaming of going back to India in order to die there.[8] In his memoirs Karl Wilhelm referred to Princess Bamba as 'the true heiress of Ranjit Singh', meaning that she was most conscious of the actual desperate situation of the whole family. 'She considered the Punjab and Kashmir as the lost possession of her family and was absolutely furious when the border between Pakistan and India was drawn right across the Punjab.' In Princess Bamba's eyes Pakistan and India did not exist; there was just the Punjab and its capital Lahore.

She would often call in at the municipal offices at the Guildhall in Thetford to inspect her brother's portrait collection, and at the same time reprimand the staff. 'I would walk with her to the Guildhall so that she could satisfy herself that the portraits were still on display,' remembers the town clerk. The staff did not look forward to her irregular visits. By the 1950s the rooms where the paintings were displayed were being used for public functions, dances and other events, and the collection was not very safe there. Paintings were being damaged and in some cases stolen from Prince Frederick's collection. Around 1954 they were removed to an attic for safe storage because of damage from smoke pollution and vandalism, but the damp and unventilated conditions only caused further deterioration. In 1956 Princess Bamba unexpectedly visited the Guildhall. She was not amused. 'My brother gave these portraits to the town on condition they are displayed so people can see them,'[9] she fumed.

Princess Catherine and Princess Bamba with their ponies, photographed outside the entrance of Elveden Hall, *c.* 1882. Both sisters, together with their brothers Princes Victor and Frederick, were keen riders.

Princess Bamba's coming of age, dressed for her formal presentation at Court, *c.* 1892. Following the death of her mother, Princess Bamba enrolled at Somerville Hall School, Oxford, with her sister Princess Catherine. While Catherine passed all her examinations, Princess Bamba was not so assiduous in her studies, poor in French prose and translation, but she succeeded in grammar. At the end of the term the sisters came back from Oxford to London where they passed their time by going to concerts and operas.

The Manor House at Old Buckenham, *c.* 1900. Princess Bamba and her sisters resided at the Manor House from 1897, while their brother Prince Frederick was at Old Buckenham Hall. In 1909 Princess Bamba and her sisters moved down to Blo Norton with Prince Frederick. The family had a lot of baggage, as their previous homes were much larger. Local villagers assisted in the move and huge wooden cases of furniture and household items were temporarily stored in barns.

The tomb of Maharajah Ranjit Singh, *c.* 1870. Princess Bamba made a special family trip to India with her husband and her sister Princess Sophia in 1924. She visited the shrine of her grandmother, the Maharani Jind Kaur, at Nasik, where she had been cremated in 1864. Here, with the assistance of the Kapurthala State Authorities,[10] the Princess had her grandmother's remains removed and placed beside the tomb of Maharajah Ranjit Singh at Lahore, in a small ceremony on 17 March 1924. The prayers were offered by Harbans Singh, a descendant of the Sikh warrior Sham Singh Atariwala.[11]

Princess Bamba wearing a white sari in Kashmir, *c.* 1924. While in India, Princess Bamba's letters began to echo a tone heard some forty years before from France. 'I have been very ill, in bed for nine weeks! It has left me with great weakness of the eyes.' Then she added the twist: 'I was poisoned just the night before I came into Kashmir, this is not the first time by any means, that I have been poisoned by the CID!'[12] It was obvious from Foreign Office files that she was being watched. It seemed history was repeating itself. 'Whilst I was in Delhi I wrote to the Secretary of State, of course nothing will come of it, I had to give them a piece of my mind, I said amongst other things, if they gave "Independence", it would automatically revert to me',[13] she wrote.

Princess Bamba visiting Khalsa College, Amritsar, during the 1940s received by Sunder Singh Ramgarhia (centre). In 1944 Princess Bamba shifted from The Gulzar to 104 Block A, Model Town in Lahore,[14] where she again made trouble sending letters to the Secretary General of the United Nations. The Foreign Office maintained their surveillance. Her pleas, however, were falling on deaf ears. All her mail was censored, as she was fully aware. However, after Indian independence and the subsequent partition of the Punjab, Princess Bamba's fiery letters to the government ceased. Her visits to India and the newly formed Pakistan also became more frequent, while her health continued to decline.

Hampton House, the Princesses' Norfolk residence in Blo Norton. In 1935 the sisters began to vacate Blo Norton Hall, as the lease had expired. Most of their effects were moved down the street to Hampton House, a thatched house with about 2 acres of land with cowsheds at the rear. The Princess had also hired some land further down the village so that her cows could graze from time to time, while her gardener, Mr Declan, was kept busy with the garden's avenue of roses and beautiful lawns with apple, cherry and pear trees. The driveway at Blo Norton and Penn was nothing short of a classic car showroom, with a Daimler and a Ford VA Pilot parked alongside a stunning cream open-topped 1929 Buick convertible.[15] The American Buick was a real eye-catcher and Princess Bamba would be seen chauffeured at high speeds, an experience she apparently loved.

Princess Bamba on a picnic with Mrs Ivy Lane, *c.* 1938. In stature she was a tiny woman, with a limp from an accident, and she became rather grumpy in her old age, as well as a bit eccentric. She got her servants to encourage bees to bite her to cure her rheumatism, while moaning about the Germans. 'German women have such big backsides, that's why they have big armchairs in Germany,' she would chant, and even refused to have Wagner played in the house, although she adored opera.[16] She just loved to be awkward, bathing in her bedroom so the servants had to carry pots of hot water up the stairs. She refused electricity at Hampton House, and even insisted that the cables were run around the back garden to prevent their crossing in front of the house.

Sardar Beant Singh Sandhawalia, the eldest living member of the Sandhawalia family in 1950. Beant Singh accompanied his father Pritam Singh on his last few visits to Princess Bamba in Lahore after the partition of India. He recalled how on each occasion the Princess' health declined rapidly. In 1955 Karim Baksh wrote to Pritam Singh, 'Her Highness Princess Bamba is well but very weak, her hand shakes and she cannot write'[17] – her last few letters were just initialled or in her servant Karim Baksh's hand. A neighbour in Lahore recalled, 'Old Princess Sutherland, the last descendant of Maharajah Ranjit Singh, complained that she could not get a seat on the bus, when all Punjab should have been hers! The old lady spent her days dreaming about her ancestral glory.'[18] On 10 March 1957 the Princess died of heart failure, at the age of eighty-nine. She had outlived her entire family and the final chapter of a tragic family was finally laid to rest. Her funeral was conducted in a Christian ceremony at Lahore, her rites witnessed by a select few Pakistani dignitaries. But due to the sensitive relations between India and Pakistan at the time, there were sadly no Sikhs present.

11

The Legacy of Maharajah Duleep Singh

Elveden Hall, c. 1900, after refurbishment by the Iveagh family.

Driving up the old A11 to Elveden has never been easier. In the days of the old Maharajah, it must have been a tricky task travelling through the heavy Victorian fog with dim carriage lighting, along oil-lamp-lit streets dotted with inns or stop houses, but the warm fire-lit Elveden Hall was surely a splendour which shone from afar. Today, the roadside Saxon church of St Andrew and St Patrick, where the graves of the Maharajah, his wife, and his young son lie in the churchyard, is the only sight that catches the eye when passing the village of Elveden. The moss-covered marble headstones surrounded by overgrown pasture are a sad reminder of the last son of the Sarkar Khalsa.

After the Maharajah's death, Maharani Ada often visited the family back in England, and on many occasions would be seen travelling around in Europe with Prince Victor, who had taken a liking to her. During the First World War Ada drove a French Red Cross ambulance at the Battle of Verdun, but in 1919 she returned to London with debts of £17,000. She settled at Madeira Park in Tunbridge Wells, and led a very quiet life, passing her time writing letters to the India Office to increase her funds and even asked for a loan to open her own hat shop. During her final days she also took up residence at 27 Grosvenor Place, London, and on 6 August the last Maharani of the Punjab passed away at the age of sixty-one. She left her entire estate to her daughter Pauline Torry, including her £20,000 life insurance with Phoenix Assurance, which she left in a trust to Pauline in the care of Messrs Coutts & Co. The funeral was held at Golders Green crematorium on 9 August 1930, and the service conducted by the Reverend Herbert Trundle. Maharani Ada's only surviving daughter, Princess Pauline, and her step-daughter, Princess Sophia, were the chief mourners. Princesses Catherine and Bamba declined to attend – the latter would go to her grave believing that Ada was the British spy planted on her late father. Ada's companion Nurse Spain and the loyal family solicitor Harold Farrer were present among neighbours from Madeira Park. For a queen, the service was a small affair and passed by without a mention in the press.

On Prince Victor's death in 1918, all his real and personal estate was left to his wife Lady Anne Blanche. His only wish was that a sapphire ring given to him by the Earl of Carnarvon be bequeathed to the said Earl's son Lord Porchester, to be preserved as an heirloom and passed on with the Carnarvon estate. In his will, Prince Victor requested that his wife wore no mourning on his account, and he desired to be cremated. His wife, however, arranged for the Prince's burial in preference to a cremation. Prince Victor spent most of his young life in London's West End, from Mount Street to Portland Place, his only Norfolk home being the impressive Hockwold Hall, a hunting lodge since the eighteenth century, the existence of which is recorded in Domesday Book. The house is much associated with Queen Victoria who stayed there when she visited her favourite godson. Today the Hall is in private hands, and annually hosts the Hockwold country fair.

After the death of Prince Victor, Lady Anne, or Princess Victor as she preferred to be called, spent most of her time in Paris, where she was well known in society, making only seasonal visits to her family in England.[1] When her husband died, she returned the remaining family jewels in her late husband's possession to Prince Frederick. On the outbreak of the Second World War, Lady Anne retained an unshakeable belief that Britain and the Allies would eventually win. She had the opportunity to return to England during 1939/40 but refused to do so saying that France was her adopted country and that she would stay there just as she had during the First World War. During the occupation of France she steadfastly refused to either fraternise or collaborate with the Germans. As a British subject she was interned in a camp at Besançon towards the end of 1940, where she experienced much hardship. However, she was released early in 1941 as being over-age. During the remainder of the war, having very little money, she sold a portion of her very valuable jewellery to provide a subsistence-level income for herself, her servants and other less fortunate friends. Parts of the proceeds were given through intermediaries to finance resistance cells. Lady Anne was a 'courageous and unusual woman' and was later awarded the Médaille de la Reconnaissance Française and the Médaille de la France Libérée for her outstanding services during the war.[2] After the Second World War she continued to live in Paris, but every summer she would go to stay at Pirton Court in Worcester with her sister-in-law, Lady Deerhurst. Her life in Paris became somewhat quieter but many French friends and English relations would come and visit her. Her life-long interest was horse racing, about which she was knowledgeable and successful. Over the years her horses won many races on the Paris racecourses, and her many friends therefore were from the racing fraternity – the Aga Khan, the Rothschilds and Boussac. The most famous of her horses was Kerbela, who won about fifteen races.

Princess Catherine's wish was to be cremated, and, on her death, her sister Princess Sophia, who was her trustee, made the necessary arrangements at north London's Golders Green crematorium. Princess Catherine left all her jewellery and personal effects to be divided between her two sisters and added a codicil to her will, when her life-long confidante passed away before her, stating, 'I wish three quarters of my ashes to be buried at Elveden churchyard and about one quarter of the ashes to be put in a casket and buried as near as possible to the coffin of my friend Fräulein Schafer at the Principal Cemetery at Kassel in Germany.' Princess Catherine's entire life was shrouded in mystery, but fifty-five years after her death a new mystery arose. A dormant Swiss bank account in her name, as well as one in the name of her governess, came to light. Rumours and speculation mounted surrounding its existence and contents, but in 2002 it was given to the family of Pir Karim.

Princess Sophia was also cremated at Golders Green crematorium and her ashes were later taken by Princess Bamba to India. Her detailed will gives an insight into how generous and thoughtful a person she was. She left various pieces of her Indian jewellery to her friends and servants, including her goddaughter Mrs Nancy Pink; the sum of £300 was given to the Sikh girls' school in Ferozepore, Punjab; £500 to the Battersea dogs' home; £100 to the Indian Women's Education Association; and she also left £200 each to a Mohammedan and Hindu girls' school in the Punjab to be chosen by the trustees. In addition, all servants past and present were given generous sums, including Princess Sophia's godchild Chrystal Calvert who received £100. The princess added 'To Eton College three hundred pounds for the upkeep of the memorial garden there to my brother . . .', while the rectors of Elveden and Blo Norton received £150 each for the maintenance of the church and her family's graves. Her adopted son Pritam Singh Sandhawalia received £300 and her brother-in-law Pierre Villemont was left £200, while the portrait of Maharajah Duleep Singh by Partridge, which Lady Login had saved, was given to the Lahore Museum. Princess Sophia also gave the Inverness Museum her brother Prince Frederick's collection of Jacobite Stuart relics, which she had loaned them, and which were now to be placed permanently with their Stuart collection.

The graves in Elveden church, *c.* 1900. Zooming along the same stretch of road today, you can very easily miss the once flamboyant Elveden Hall, barely visible through the wild and overgrown estate woodland, which was once the heart of the gaming paradise in Britain. In winter, when the naked trees have shed their leaves, glimpses of the now domed Hall can be spotted. The graves in the church were formerly sealed in by iron railings, but these were removed in 1959 with the consent of the authorities, after a petition by the Reverend C.J. Newton Agates, the rector of Elveden, in order that the graves could 'be kept tidy which was impossible under existing circumstances'.

Dosanjh (right), a Sikh soldier in the British Army, with a fellow British officer and a Gurkha visiting Duleep Singh's grave in 1934. The grave is now a visiting site for many thousands of Sikhs settled in Britain, Europe and even as far afield as the Punjab. They come to pay homage to the last Sikh monarch who, however grand himself, was unable to reach and touch the soil of the 'land of five rivers'.[3] The graves at Elveden have become a centrepiece, together with the recently unveiled bronze statue at Button Island of Maharajah Duleep Singh mounted on a horse, and a lasting memorial of the first Sikh settler. Sikhs flock here all year round offering their prayers and leaving a token of goodwill.

Elveden Hall, 2003. Today Elveden Hall and its surrounding village is quieter than ever before. There are no more extravagant pheasant shoots or great hunts. The green domed Hall lies abandoned by its century-old masters. The interior marble halls which echo the memories of a once regal resident still show signs of the American Air Force stationed here. US bomber pilot Harry Crosby described arriving at the Third Air Division headquarters at Elveden Hall in 1943: 'At Elveden Hall I was in a palace, home of one of the richest Maharajahs of India.'[4] The Hall, which is not open to the public and is on private land, can be vividly seen within the stone wall boundary of the adjoining Elveden church. The Iveaghs extended Elveden Hall in 1901, doubling its original size by removing the servants' quarters, which could be seen to the left of the Hall. The dome was added with further oriental marble decorations.

The Iveagh family, who purchased the estate in 1894, used the Hall as their residence for over forty years, and allowed it to be used as a US airbase during the Second World War, after which time it was completely boarded up. In 1984 the Hall was reopened by the then Lord Iveagh for the first time in many years for the grand sale of contents. Private buyers and dealers as well as curious Sikhs arrived at this exotic location together with many local folk who simply wanted to catch a glimpse of this Indian palace. The full glory of the Hall was restored for the course of the sale. Persian rugs, antique silver and magnificent oils could be seen hanging over the rich marble walls. The sale fetched in excess of six million pounds, much more than was expected. There were not many relics of its former Sikh resident – only a large copy of the Winterhalter painting by Janet Hawkins and a *Spy* cartoon of Duleep Singh. After the sale the doors once again closed, with the memory of the Maharajah again shut within its walls.

The Maharajah's London residence at Holland Park. Today Mulgrave Castle in Whitby is in private hands while Hatherop Castle in Gloucestershire is part of the Ernest Cook Trust. The London house rented by the Maharajah at Holland Park is also a private home, and is now surrounded by many international embassies. Among the earlier Scottish homes of Maharajah Duleep Singh, Castle Menzies in Perthshire is today a tourist attraction run by the Menzies Charitable Trust, while Auchlyne House and Loch Kennard Lodge still remain tenanted retreats.

Kenmore church in Perthshire, Scotland. The nearby church at Kenmore is the peaceful resting-place of the Maharajah's first child who died soon after birth. His large gravestone carries the inscription 'To the Memory of the Infant Son of the Maharajah Duleep Singh, Late Ruler of the Sikh Nation, Punjab, India and the Maharanee his Wife, born 4th August 1865, died 5th August 1865', and is situated at the rear of the churchyard.

Maharani Jind Kaur's residence at Lancaster Gate. On her death the Maharani's personal wealth was pitiful – a meagre £12,000,[5] compared to the riches she once possessed. Probate was granted on 6 November 1893 to 'The Maharajah Duleep Singh of Hatherop Castle, in the County of Gloucester, the natural and lawful son and only next to kin of the deceased'. The Maharani's first residence in England, 1 Lancaster Gate, was referred to as 'number one round-the-corner', as its entrance, unlike the other houses on the street, was from the side, this being the first house in a U-shaped street, with Christ church in the centre. At that time these were the only houses at Lancaster Gate – the properties facing Kensington Gardens were built a few years later. When these whitewashed houses were completed, the numbers changed, and today the house lived in by Maharani Jind Kaur is 23 Lancaster Gate. Abingdon House on Wrights Lane in Kensington (now known as Marloes Road) was the Maharani's final home, but it was demolished to build a square of new houses called Cheniston Gardens.

The graves of Prince Victor Duleep Singh and Lady Anne Blanche in Monaco. Lady Anne Duleep Singh died on 2 July 1956 and was buried at her wish beside her husband in the Cimetière de Monaco. Their graves are in a joint tomb high on the hills of Monte Carlo, overlooking the Mediterranean Sea. Her total estate in England amounted to £46,145, of which she bequeathed part to one of her executors, General Louis Joseph Francis Rene Hary, and part to the then Earl of Coventry. Generous amounts were also distributed between her servants, while her friends received clothes and jewels.

The present Old Buckenham Hall. Prince Frederick's Georgian country house, was sold in 1906, and bought by a rich Australian stockbroker, Lionel Robinson, who loved cricket. The grounds behind the Hall were turned into a cricket club, where some private test matches were known to have been played. A game between an Australian touring side and an England XI was watched by a large crowd of Norfolk folk in 1921. The Sewell family bought Old Buckenham Hall in 1936 and converted it into a private boarding preparatory school, but a fire in 1952 put an end to the school and the grand building. It is now a modest private country house, with only faint memories of Prince Frederick: the once fine grounds contain a plaque erected by Prince Frederick to commemorate Queen Victoria's Diamond Jubilee and at Old Buckenham itself there is an old oak tree planted by the Prince at the junction of the village, known as the 'Black Prince's Tree'.[6]

Breckles House. Prince Frederick only stayed a short while at Breckles House, which is now a privately owned cottage. His home is often mistakenly assumed to be Breckles Hall, which is the much grander château-like residence not far away. The Hall was the home of the Montague family, and one of its famous residents is said to have been Sir Winston Churchill.

Blo Norton Hall. Entering Blo Norton today from the A1066 one could never imagine that the royal descendants of the Maharajah of the Punjab once adorned this quiet and sleepy Norfolk village. On the left is a small fenced area bequeathed by Prince Frederick to the National Trust; on the right is the Princesses' Hampton House. Further down at the junction is the parish church with Prince Frederick's grave, then the Hall and finally the Prince's temple. Blo Norton Hall is now privately tenanted, with a moat and splendid acres of woodland and picturesque gardens.

Blo Norton church. The walls of this little medieval church still give a tantalising feeling of Prince Frederick's love for this parish. A marble plaque opposite the church doors as you enter is inscribed, 'To The Memory of His Highness Prince Frederick Victor Duleep Singh MVO, 3rd son of their Highnesses the Maharajah and Maharanee of Lahore, born 23rd January 1868, died 15 August 1926'. The plaque mistakenly describes Prince Frederick as the third son of the Maharajah, whereas he was the second (if one excludes the infant son who died after one day). Beside the door there is also a beautiful manuscript roll-of-honour, containing the name of Prince Frederick halfway down the list.

Prince Frederick's gravestone, Blo Norton churchyard. The church bells were restored some years ago with the help of a generous donation from a Sikh community. Prince Frederick's grave is now sadly neglected and little known to the outside world, situated on the far right of the churchyard as you enter from the main gates. The stone's barely visible inscription reads 'In Memory of Prince Frederick Duleep Singh, second son of the late Maharajah and Maharani Duleep Singh, born January 23rd 1868, died August 15th 1926'. In his will, Prince Frederick left £100 to his sister-in-law Princess Anne Duleep Singh while his stepmother Maharani Ada received £200. Princess Pauline was left one quarter of the life insurance money received from Phoenix Life, and the remaining three quarters was shared among his three sisters and other stepsister Princess Irene. Every single servant in the service of Prince Frederick was left a small legacy and his will closed by stating that 'all personal estate whatsoever was to be divided between my three sisters Princesses Bamba, Catherine and Sophia'.

The Ancient House Museum in Thetford. On Prince Frederick's death his vast collection of Norfolk portraits was displayed in the Guildhall at Thetford, and today some are at the town hall. Founded by Prince Frederick, the Ancient House Museum has a room dedicated to the life of the Duleep Singhs, housing personal artefacts of the family, including the lavish Bible given by Dalhousie, family photographs and also Prince Frederick's full yeomanry uniform.

Blo Norton War memorial. After the First World War Prince Frederick paid his tribute to the men who had laid down their lives, and designed a beautiful war memorial. It is a slender and graceful monument with a tall cross on a pedestal around which are carved and painted the arms of special interest to the parish. Prince Frederick unveiled the memorial on 7 November 1920 outside the churchyard of Blo Norton parish church.

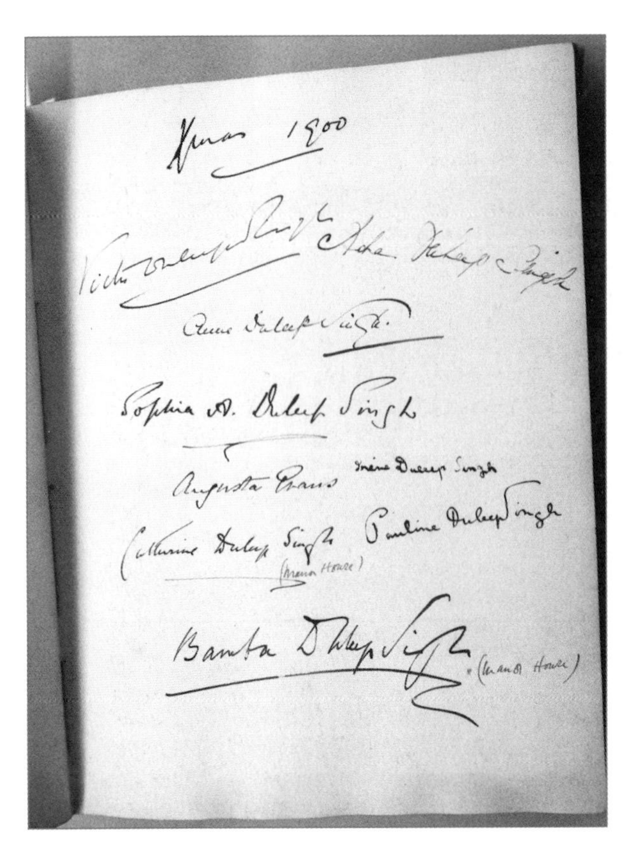
Xmas 1900

Sophia A. Duleep Singh

Irene Duleep Singh

Pauline Duleep Singh

Bamba Duleep Singh

A page from the Old Buckenham Hall visitors' book. The entry for Christmas 1900 shows the signatures of Prince Victor, Maharani Ada, Lady Anne Blanche, Princess Sophia, Princess Irene, Princess Catherine, Princess Pauline and Princess Bamba. Very little is known of the Maharajah's children from his second marriage, Princesses Irene and Pauline, as they led isolated lives. In the winter of 1892 the Maharajah and Maharani Ada took a holiday to Algiers with Prince Victor and Prince Frederick, where Princesses Pauline and Irene were baptised in the Christian faith. In 1914 Princess Pauline married J.S.A. Torry, 2nd Lieutenant of the 12th Battalion Rifle Brigade, but he died of wounds in the Battle of Loos on 19 September 1915. She had befriended Princess Sophia, and would often visit the family in Norfolk. Her stays at Old Buckenham Hall were well recorded in the visitors' book there,[7] but her death in France during the Second World War was unrecorded.

This is the only known photograph of Princess Irene Duleep Singh, *c.* 1910. She is escorting the wealthy businessman Arthur Brown around the Pyramids in Cairo, and Mrs C. Dew Carey and Mrs Carey's daughter are seated behind her. Princess Irene married Pierre Marie Villament, in Paris on 15 March 1910. However, she led a very troubled life and, according to the Nice correspondent of the *Petit Pariser*, was a neurasthenic, and made an attempt to end her life in 1925 by throwing herself from a window after separating from her husband in August: tragically, on 8 October 1926 local fishermen dragged her body out of the sea near Monte Carlo. A year earlier she had been treated in a nursing home in England for the same disorder, but later moved back to Paris where she took up painting. She was apparently much aggrieved by the death of her half-brother Prince Frederick, who had died two months earlier. The *Morning Post* quoted Princess Irene as being 'tired of life', and a verdict of suicide was given.[8]

The grave of Princess Bamba Sutherland. The last member of the Duleep Singh family, Princess Bamba is buried in the Christian Cemetery in Lahore. On her death in Lahore her entire estate was left to Mr Pir Karim Baksh Supra. The property in England was disposed of by the government – including her home at Hilden Hall in Penn, where the authorities appointed a local house clearance firm, run by a father and son. The son recalled how the house was extremely lavish, and how furniture and personal belongings were piled up and burnt, while possessions of any value were sold off. In Lahore, Pir Karim Baksh Supra sold the stunning oil and portraiture collection – a total of eighty-seven items – to the Lahore Fort Museum. The exquisite collection of photographs, paintings and personal artefacts now forms the Princess Bamba Collection.

Sardar Beant Singh Sandhawalia in February 2001, his son Sukhdev Singh Sandhawalia standing behind. Today the Sandhawalia family still reside in Amritsar. Beant Singh, aged seventy-seven, still has fond memories of visits to Princess Bamba in Lahore and her earlier visits to Amritsar. His son Sukhdev Singh is actively involved in promoting Sikhism and its heritage, organising educational groups and running a Sikh magazine.

Maharajah Duleep Singh Family Tree

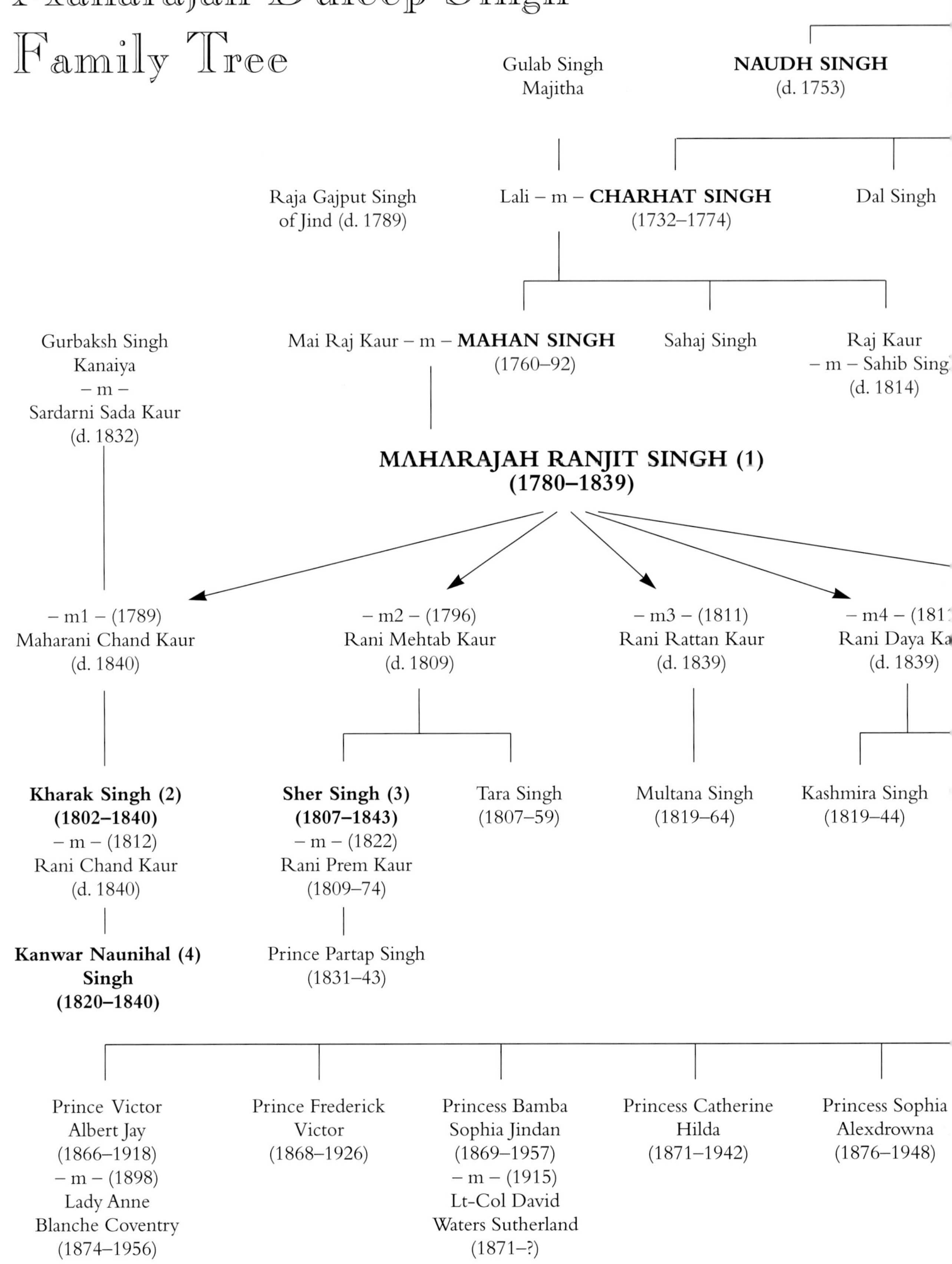

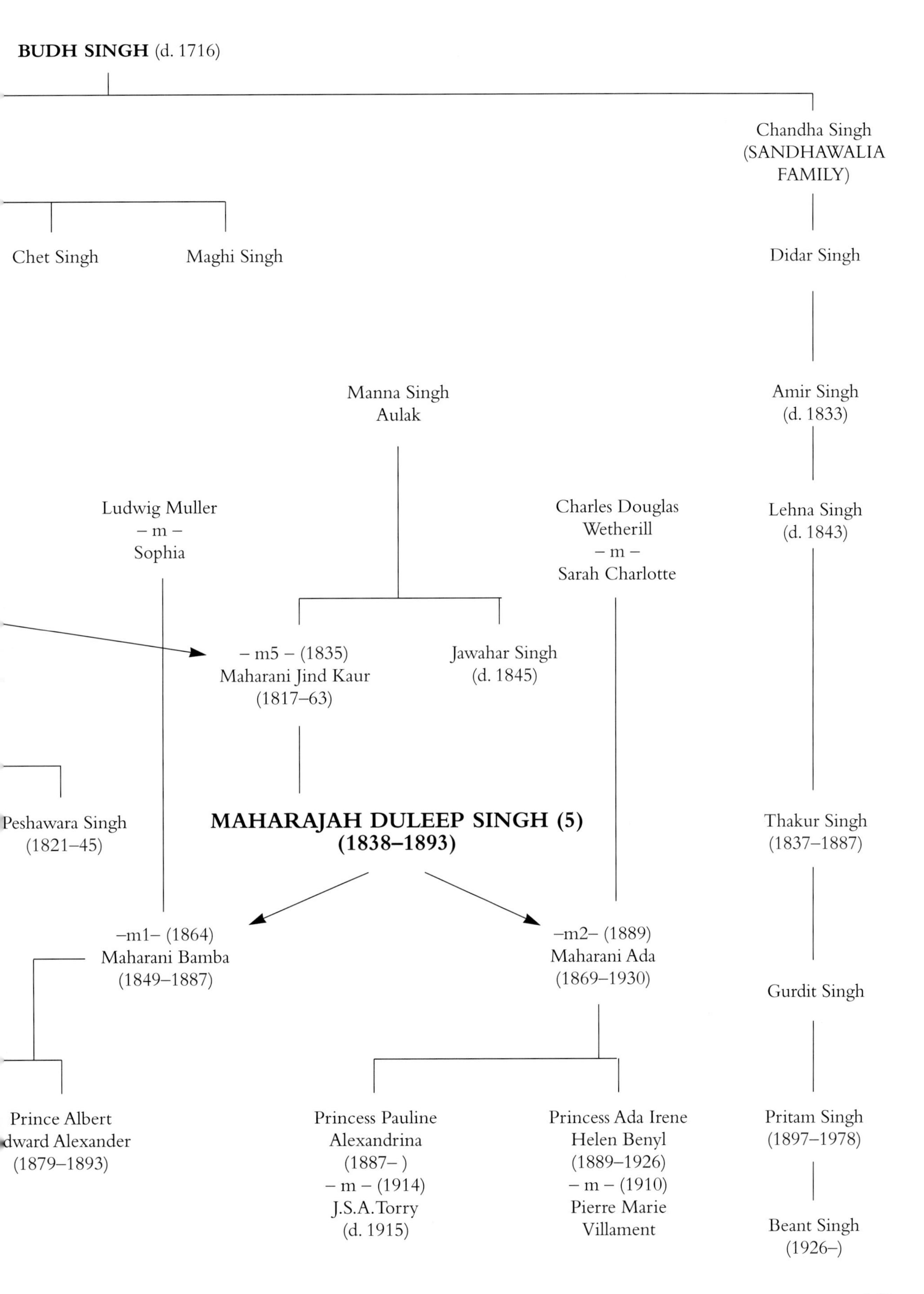
BUDH SINGH (d. 1716)
Chandha Singh (SANDHAWALIA FAMILY)
Chet Singh
Maghi Singh
Didar Singh
Manna Singh Aulak
Amir Singh (d. 1833)
Ludwig Muller – m – Sophia
Charles Douglas Wetherill – m – Sarah Charlotte
Lehna Singh (d. 1843)
– m5 – (1835) Maharani Jind Kaur (1817–63)
Jawahar Singh (d. 1845)
Peshawara Singh (1821–45)
MAHARAJAH DULEEP SINGH (5) (1838–1893)
Thakur Singh (1837–1887)
–m1– (1864) Maharani Bamba (1849–1887)
–m2– (1889) Maharani Ada (1869–1930)
Gurdit Singh
Prince Albert dward Alexander (1879–1893)
Princess Pauline Alexandrina (1887–) – m – (1914) J.S.A.Torry (d. 1915)
Princess Ada Irene Helen Benyl (1889–1926) – m – (1910) Pierre Marie Villament
Pritam Singh (1897–1978)
Beant Singh (1926–)

Glossary

Bol-so-nihal	First part of the Sikh war-cry, meaning 'anyone who speaks will be happy'. The second part to the war-cry is *Sat Sri Akal*, which means 'that the immortal God is true'
Durbar	Royal Court
Gurmukhi	The Sikh script of the Punjabi language
Guru Granth Sahib	Sikh Holy text
Jat	Farmer
Kalghi	Plume; turban ornament
Kanwar	Crown Prince; heir-apparent
Karewa	A ceremony of marriage by placing a shawl over the bride's head
Khalsa	Pure; a Sikh Order founded by the tenth Guru, Gobind Singh, on 13 April 1699
Lakh	One hundred thousand
Lascar	Indian sailor
Misal	Confederacy, formation of rule used by Sikhs in the eighteenth century
Mohammedan	Muslim, a follower of Mohammed
Pahul	The sweet water taken in the initiation ceremony of a Khalsa Sikh
Pind	Village
Pundit	Priest
Rakhi	A system of protection money used by the Misal leaders
Rani	Queen
Samadh	Tomb or a memorial built at place of cremation
Sardar	Chief or headperson
Sarkar	Governing body. Ranjit Singh preferred to be called *Sarkar Khalsa* rather than Maharajah
Toshkhanna	Royal treasury
Zenana	Female establishment for the wives of the Maharajah

References

Introduction

1 C. Smyth, *The Reigning Family of Lahore* (London, Thacker & Co., 1847), p. 14.
2 There were twelve Misals, namely (1) Kaniaya, (2) Sukarchakia, (3) Shaheed, (4) Phulkian, (5) Bhangi, (6) Dhalewal, (7) Nishanwala, (8) Nakkai, (9) Alhuwalia, (10) Ramgarhia, (11) Karorasinghia, (12) Faizalpuria.
3 The Rakhi system worked by offering villagers security and protection from outside plunderers and looters such as the Afghan Durranis and even break-away Mughal factions.
4 Jind at the time was a small independent Phulkian state under the rule of Raja Gajput Singh.
5 S.L. Suri, *Umdat Ut Tiwarikh 1885–89* (Lahore, Arya Press, 1961).
6 The former two men were from the Bhangi Misal.
7 Sialkot is now in the Punjab province of Pakistan.
8 H. Pearse, *Soldier and Traveller: The Memoirs of Alexander Gardner* (Edinburgh, Blackwood, 1898), p. 253.
9 Smyth, *Reigning Family*, p. 99.
10 Ibid., p. 100.
11 J.D. Cunningham, *History of the Sikhs from the Origin of the Nation to the Battles of the Sutlej* (London, John Murray, 1849), p. 258.
12 G. Singh, *Maharajah Duleep Singh Correspondence* (Patiala, Punjabi University, 1977), p. 51.
13 *Broughton Collection preserved in the Punjab State Archives* (Patiala), Letter from Hardinge to Hobhouse, dated 4 December 1847.
14 *Broughton Collection*, Governor General to Henry Lawrence, 16 August 1847.
15 G. Singh, *Maharajah Duleep Singh*, p. 55.
16 Ibid., p. 52.
17 Chattar Singh had fallen out with the British as they refused the marriage of his daughter with Maharajah Duleep Singh, which had been arranged some years earlier.

Chapter 1

1 Nankhana Sahib is the birthplace of Guru Nanak, while Nanded is where Guru Gobind Singh was cremated.
2 Deriving the name of a newborn from the Sikh Granth is a common Sikh practice.
3 The town was Duleepgarh.
4 L.H. Griffin, *Rulers of India: Ranjit Singh and the Sikh Barrier between our growing Empire and Central Asia* (London, OUP, 1916), p. 106.
5 Suri, *Umdat ut Tiwarikh*, p. 525.
6 In the district of Farukhabad, state of Uttar Pradesh, India.
7 D. Singh, *The Maharajah Duleep Singh and the Government* (London, Trubner & Co., 1884), p. 77.
8 L. Login, *Sir John Login and Duleep Singh* (London, W.H. Allen, 1890), p. 159.
9 The painting remained in the Dalhousie estate for many years, until it was sold by Lady Broun Lindsay at the Colstoun Sale of 1990.
10 D. Singh, *Maharajah Duleep Singh*, p. 81.
11 Ibid., p. 79.
12 J. Kennedy, *Maharajah Duleep Singh*, Christian Treasury (1854), pp. 511–13.
13 Ibid., p. 512.
14 The portrait forms part of the Princess Bamba Collection at the Lahore Fort Museum, Pakistan.
15 British Library, *India Office Collection*, Letters from Bibi Jind Kaur to Lawrence.
16 *Illustrated London News*, 30 June 1849.
17 Login, *Sir John Login*, p. 158.
18 E.D. Login, *Lady Login's Recollections* (London, John Murray, 1916), p. 206.
19 One *lakh rupees* was equivalent to £10,000.
20 Login, *Sir John Login*, pp. 182–3.
21 M. Alexander & S. Anand, *Queen Victoria's Maharajah: Duleep Singh 1838–1893* (London, Weidenfeld & Nicolson, 1980), p. 14.
22 Login, *Sir John Login*, p. 297.
23 Login, *Lady Login's Recollections*, p. 89.

Chapter 2

1 Ma-Bap, meaning mother-father.
2 Login, *Sir John Login*, p. 230.
3 Alexander, *Victoria's Maharajah*, p. 39.
4 Login, *Sir John Login*, p. 330.
5 Login, *Lady Login's Recollections*, p. 113.

6 Ibid., p. 114.
7 Later Claridges Hotel.
8 Royal Archives, *Queen Victoria's Journal*, 6 July 1854.
9 Login, *Lady Login's Recollections*, p. 114.
10 F.S. Aijazuddin, *Sikh Portraits By European Artists* (London, Sotheby Parke Bernet, 1979), p. 97.
11 D. Singh, *Maharajah Duleep Singh*, p. 86.
12 The Bible is displayed in its original form at the Ancient House Museum, Thetford.
13 The painting hangs at Osborne House, Isle of Wight. Winterhalter wanted the picture to be a permanent portrait of the young Oriental Prince, so he gave the sitter the height he judged he would attain when he reached manhood. The calculation however proved incorrect, as the Maharajah never grew any taller.
14 The original is in the Royal Collection, while the plaster cast which was displayed at Blo Norton Hall is now in the Lahore Fort Museum.
15 Login, *Lady Login's Recollections*, p. 110.
16 King Edward VII.
17 Duke of Saxe-Coburg-Gotha.
18 Alexander, *Victoria's Maharajah*, p. 53.
19 Login, *Lady Login's Recollections*, p. 116.
20 Singh, *Maharajah Duleep Singh*, p. 84.
21 Login, *Sir John Login*, p. 405.
22 Singh, *Maharajah Duleep Singh*, p. 85.
23 R. Hall, *Lovers on the Nile* (Readers Union, 1980), pp. 20–2.
24 The Maharajah is listed in Auchlyne House 'Lessees' as a tenant between 1858 and 1861.

Chapter 3

1 Login, *Lady Login's Recollections*, p. 207.
2 Login, *Sir John Login*, p. 450.
3 C. Campbell, *The Maharajah's Box* (London, HarperCollins, 2000), p. 119.
4 Login, *Sir John Login*, p. 456.
5 The house is now known as 23 Lancaster Gate. Houses on either side of Christ Church were the only ones completed then. The Maharani's house was known as 'No.1 Round-the-Corner' because the first and last houses of the U-shaped street were entered via the side and not from Lancaster Gate itself. The houses facing Kensington Gardens were built many years later.
6 Login, *Lady Login's Recollections*, p. 211.
7 This house has since been demolished to make way for Cheniston Gardens.
8 Alexander, *Victoria's Maharajah*, p. 96.
9 D. Singh, *Maharajah Duleep Singh*, p. 90.
10 Login, *Lady Login's Recollections*, p. 214.
11 A copy of this painting hangs at the Walker Art Gallery in Liverpool.
12 Duleep Singh purchased Elveden Hall on 29 September 1863.
13 Login, *Lady Login's Recollections*, p. 230.
14 Lady Login afterwards moved to St Vincent in West Malling, Kent, and later to Cedars in Aylesford where she died on 17 April 1904 aged eighty-four. She was buried beside the grave of her husband.
15 Marion Fontius, 4 May 1999.
16 Ludwig later returned to Germany, where his family still lives today.
17 There is no record or mention in family papers that a marriage took place.
18 In 1853 Ludwig Muller (1821–99) married Charlotte Ellis Eynaud, and they had nine children.
19 The local municipality demolished the memorial around 1935 to construct an outlet for sewage water. On the late Sikh historian Ganda Singh's visit in 1940 he noted that 'only a small 2½ foot pillar stood on the spot. It becomes visible in winter when the water level recedes' (G. Singh, *Maharajah Duleep Singh*, p. 93).
20 Login, *Lady Login's Recollections*, p. 237.
21 *Times of India*, 30 June 1864.

Chapter 4

1 G. Lacelles, *Thirty-Five Years in the Forest* (London, Edward Arnold, 1915).
2 J.E. Borch, *The Blue Hare; Hare Hawking in the 19th Century* (London, 1896).
3 J. Osgood, *Uncensored Recollections*, 2nd edn (London, Nash & Grayson, 1924), p. 248.
4 J.H. Coke, *Tracks of a Rolling Stone* (London, Smith Elder, 1905).
5 Duleep Singh's name is erased from the Carlton Club membership book.
6 Royal Archives, *Burnes to Ponsonby*, 22 June 1883, f. N2/42.
7 D. Shaw, *London in the Sixties by One of the Old Brigade* (London, Everett & Co, 1914), p. 168.
8 Royal Archives, *Ponsonby to Prince of Wales*, 4 April 1891.
9 Lady Login also mentioned an opera that the Maharajah was working on but could not recall the title.
10 Aijauzuddin, *Sikh Portraits*, p. 13.
11 Princess Bamba Collection, Lahore Fort Museum.
12 The painting remained in the Hall for over a century, and was sold by the then Lord Iveagh in the Elveden Hall sale of 1984 by Christies for £14,000.
13 Prince F. Duleep Singh, *Portraits in Norfolk Houses* (Norwich, Jarrolds, 1928), Preface by Princess Bamba Duleep Singh.

14 T.W. Turner, *Memoirs of a Gamekeeper: Elveden, 1868–1953* (London, Geoffrey Bles, 1954), p. 20.
15 Author's collection, *Letter from the Prince of Wales to R.H. Bob Collins*, dated 6 December 1876.
16 H. Gladstone, *Record Bags and Shooting Records*, 2nd edn (London, H.F. Whitherby, 1930).
17 Alexander, *Victoria's Maharajah*, p. 112.
18 Turner, *Memoirs*, p. 20.
19 Ibid., p. 100.
20 Ibid., p. 101.
21 Shaw, *London in the Sixties*, p. 259.
22 Turner, *Memoirs*, p. 24.
23 The theatre burned down in 1882 but reopened two years later as the Alhambra Theatre of Varieties. It is now the Odeon Cinema, which was built in 1936.
24 *The Times*, 3 August 1882 and 8 September 1882.
25 G. Singh, *Maharajah Duleep Singh*, p. 94.
26 E. Bell, *The Annexation of the Punjahb and the Maharajah Duleep Singh* (London, Trubner, 1882).
27 Shaw, *London in the Sixties*, p. 259.
28 *Vanity Fair* 'Spy' cartoon, *The Maharajah*, 18 November 1882.
29 G. Singh, *Maharajah Duleep Singh Correspondence*, p. 96.
30 Thakur Singh was the son of Lehna Singh Sandhawalia who had avenged the killings of Naunihal Singh in 1841 by assassinating Maharajah Sher Singh.
31 Campbell, *Maharajah's Box*, p. 75.

Chapter 5

1 The Sikh Temple *Takht Hazur Singh* is at Abchal Nagar, Nanded, which marks the spot where the tenth Sikh Guru was cremated.
2 Singh, *Maharajah Duleep Singh Correspondence*, p. 98.
3 Ibid., p. 251.
4 Not to be confused with Thakur Sing Sandhawalia. Thakur Singh Wagah was a grandson of Maharani Jind Kaur's sister.
5 G. Singh, *Maharajah Duleep Singh Correspondence*, Letter from Duleep Singh to Viceroy, dated 12 May 1886, p. 304.
6 Ibid., p. 305.
7 Pahul is taken in the presence of five Sikhs.
8 G. Singh, *Maharajah Duleep Singh Correspondence*, Resident to Viceroy, 29 May 1886, p. 333.
9 British Library, *India Office Records*, Letter from Viceroy to Resident at Aden, dated 30 May 1886.
10 Ada Douglas Wetheril was born on 15 January 1869 at 10 Oval Road, Kennington in Surrey to Charles Douglas Wetherill, and Sarah Charlotte of Bishopstoke, Hampshire. Charles was a civil engineer while his wife Sarah worked at the Phoenix gasworks at Kennington. The family moved to 41 Great Ormond Street in Holborn, London in 1881, while Ada, aged thirteen, took employment as a domestic servant at a house in Easingwold, Yorkshire. Ada later carried on her domestic work at Cox's Hotel, in west London, where she was first acquainted with Duleep Singh. She would have been around seventeen years old. In 1886 Ada met up with the Maharajah in Paris; her mother Sarah had moved to Greeminorm, and her father Charles had died leaving behind a second daughter.
11 Osgood, *Uncensored Recollections*, p. 245.
12 G. Singh, *Maharajah Duleep Singh Correspondence*, p. 404.
13 Tevis was born in Philadelphia in 1828. After resigning in 1850 from the Carlisle Barracks in Pennsylvania he offered his services to the Sultan of Turkey. He was appointed to the rank of Major and later awarded the Crimea medal by Britain. After a short return to the US, then to Rome and Switzerland, giving service to the Khedive of Egypt, he returned to Turkey. In 1865 Tevis was appointed adjutant general to General Thomas Sweeny, secretary of war of the Irish Republic and commander in chief of the Irish Republican Army. In January 1866 he was the armourer for the doomed Fenian raid in Canada. A year later he sent HM Consul in Washington a full breakdown of Fenian arms dumps in the US. The Consul noted Tevis was anxious to be an agent to HMG, he had asked for £100 per month. General Tevis died in Paris on 29 September 1900.
14 Public Records Office, Foreign Office, f. 5/1932.
15 C. Vento, *Les Salons de Paris en 1889* (Paris, 1891).
16 E.D. Cyon, *Histoire de l'Entente Franco-Russe, Mémoires et Souvenirs* (Paris, 1895).
17 London Records Office, Duleep Singh to Czar Alexander III, f. OC 10/5/1887.
18 Campbell, *Maharajah's Box*, p. 90.
19 Ibid., p. 306.
20 The exact time was noted as 4.20 a.m.
21 PRO, *OC to Foreign Office*, dated 2 May 1889, f. 26/3.
22 According to his will the Maharajah stated 'I wish to be buried wherever I may die'.

Chapter 6

1 At Eton there is a small garden dedicated to the memory of Prince Victor Duleep Singh.
2 G. Singh, *Maharajah Duleep Singh*, p. 301.

3 D. Sutherland, 'His Highness Prince Frederick Duleep Singh', *East Anglian Magazine*, September (1976), 434–7.
4 Turner, *Memoirs*, p. 22.
5 Ibid., pp. 22, 36.
6 Letters from Richard Parrott to Prince Victor Duleep Singh.
7 Author's collection, Prince Edward's Sandroyd school report.
8 PRO, OC to FO dated 19.1.1891, f. 6/33.
9 *Worcester Herald*, 5 January 1898.
10 Ibid., 5 January 1898.
11 The Robinson Library, *Gertrude Bell Archives*, letter from Gertrude Bell to her father, dated Marseilles 6 January 1905.
12 Ibid., letter from Gertrude Bell to her mother, dated Gibraltar 20 December 1905.
13 There is no photograph of Lady Anne in the Croome Archives as a young woman or of her wedding.
14 Old Buckenham Hall and Blo Norton Hall visitors' book (1897–1926).

Chapter 7

1 *Country Life*, 12 May 1906.
2 Prince F. Duleep Singh, 'Blo Norton Hall', *Norfolk & Norwich Archaeological Society Journal*, XVIII, Part 3 (19) pp. 211–61.
3 The Book Collection was donated to Thetford library.
4 The Lahore Fort Museum purchased the Schoefft collection in 1958 from Pir Karim Baksh.
5 Prince Frederick's sisters donated the items of Scottish interest to the Inverness Museum after the Second World War. The museum compiled a list in 1948.
6 Letter from Stephen Govier (1997) to the author.
7 Barbara Green, from the *Norfolk & Norwich Archaeological Society*.
8 F. Duleep Singh, *Burlington Magazine*, XI (1907).
9 F. Duleep Singh, 'A County Collection', *Connoisseur*, September (1905).
10 Letter from Mrs E. Ward to the author (1997).
11 *Norfolk Chronicle*, 'An Appreciation by Walter Rye', 20 August 1926.
12 Singh, *Norfolk Portraits*, Preface.
13 The painting was later inherited by Princess Sophia, who in her will left it to the Indian Museum at Lahore.
14 Login, *Lady Login's Recollections*, pp. 259–60.
15 The painting by S. Hall is in the Royal Collection and hangs in Osborne House.
16 *The Times*, 16.8.1926.
17 Letter from Leslie Mutum to the author.
18 *East Anglia Daily Times*, 11 September 1926.
19 This is now a private cricket club.
20 Sutherland, *Prince Frederick*, 434–7.
21 Letter from C.E. John Gaze to the author, dated 1 December 1999.
22 Sutherland, *Prince Frederick*, 434–7.
23 Pascoe Pearson, Blo Norton (1996).
24 Letter from Mrs Killingbeck (1997) to the author.
25 Letter from Kathleen Small, resident of Blo Norton between 1910–25, to the author, dated 1998.
26 The papers are part of the Iveagh Papers purchased by the Records Office at Ipswich.

Chapter 8

1 Other places visited were Peshawar, Rawalpindi, Indus, Kabul and Multan.
2 The Tank or *Sarovar* is the large body of water around the Golden Temple in Amritsar.
3 British Library, India Office Section, *Letter from Princess Catherine to Princess Sophia*, dated 20 October 1903, f. MSS E377/4.
4 British Library, India Office Section, *Letter from Princess Sophia to Princess Catherine*, f. Mss E377/4.
5 Hari Singh Nalwa who died at Jamrod, was the bravest of Ranjit Singh's Generals.
6 The *Hessische Allgemeine* newspaper, July 1997.
7 Shirley Phimister, 1999.
8 Shirley Phimister, 1999.
9 Sandhawalia family papers, *Letter to Pritam Singh from Karim Baksh*, dated 18 November 1942.
10 Golders Green crematorium, Register No. 55310.

Chapter 9

1 The piano remained in Hampton House for many years after, before it was shipped out in 1997 to the USA by the then owners.
2 The directory listed the telephone under the name of Princess Sophia, number 2219.
3 Bruce Reeve, 1997.
4 'A Princess and her Taxes': *Votes For Women*, 26 May 1911.
5 *Votes for Women*, 2 January, p. 209, *The Times*, 30 December 1913.
6 Letter dated 24 February 1916. Letter No 253, published in Omissi, *Indian Voice of the Great War*, p. 156.
7 *Calling All Women*: Newsletter of the Suffragette Fellowship, February 1949, p. 7.
8 Sandhawalia Family Papers, *Letter from Princess Sophia to Gurdit Singh*, dated 3 July 1907.
9 J. Francis, *The Tax Resistance Movement in Great Britain, Annual Reports of the WSPU*, p. 44. Courtesy of the Museum of London.

10 *Votes For Women*, 25 November 1910, p. 117.
11 Sandhawalia Family Papers, *Letter from Princess Sophia to Pritam Singh*, dated 30 October 1935.
12 Campbell, *Maharajah's Box*, pp. 17–18.
13 Sandhawalia Family Papers, *Letter from Princess Sophia to Pritam Singh*, dated 30 May 1924.
14 Mohan Singh (1897–1961) was a philanthropist and privy counsellor.
15 Sandhawalia Family Papers, *Letter from Princess Sophia to Pritam Singh*, dated 13 January 1931.
16 Later renamed Hilden Hall, presumably after Princess Catherine's middle name Hilda.
17 Now called 'Foley Meadow'.
18 Shirley Phimister, 1999.
19 Ibid., 1999.
20 Ibid., 1999.
21 Death registered at Wycombe. No. 485. Cremated at Golders Green Crematorium, Register No. 81394.
22 Last Will & Testament of P. Sophia Alexdrowna Duleep Singh, dated 29 June 1945.

Chapter 10

1 Lt-Col Sutherland MD, FRCP, MBC, was born in Buningyong, Victoria, Australia on 18 December 1871, the son of John Sutherland of Allendale, Victoria. He was educated in Melbourne and Edinburgh University, and was awarded the CIE on 3 June 1917.
2 Sandhawalia Family Papers, *Letter from K. Baksh to Pritam Singh*, dated 18 November 1942.
3 Faraday House at Hampton Court was given back to the Crown Estate Commissioners in 1955.
4 Sandhawalia Family Papers, *Letter from Princess Bamba to Pritam Singh*, no date.
5 Bruce Reeves, 1997.
6 Idem.
7 The journal, *Temple in the Woods*, 18 October 1968.
8 Karl Wilhelm Muller.
9 Ellis Clarke, *Thetford Town Clerk 1950–74*.
10 Kapurthala was a protected Sikh State in the British India, under Maharajah Jagatjit Singh.
11 Sham Singh Atariwala was the veteran Sikh General who died gallantly in the second Sikh War.
12 Sandhawalia Family Papers, *Letter from Princess Bamba to Pritam Singh*, dated 11 November 1941.
13 Sandhawalia Family Papers, *Letter from Princess Bamba to Pritam Singh*, dated 29 May 1946.
14 On 27 December 1953 Karim Baksh wrote to Pritam Singh informing him that the house was now worth only Rs.5,000.
15 The Buick was sold in 1956; the purchaser recalled the car was in mint condition with very little mileage.
16 Bruce Reeves, 1997.
17 Sandhawalia Family Papers, *Letter from Karim Baksh to Pritam Singh*, dated 11 August 1955.
18 P. Tandon, *Punjabi Century* (London, Chatto & Windus, 1961), p. 242.

Chapter 11

1 Lady Anne moved to 9 Avenue Frédéric le Play, Place de l'Ecole Militaire, Paris, where she spent the remaining years of her life.
2 C. Gordon, *The Coventrys of Croome* (Chichester, Phillimore, 2000).
3 The Punjab before its partition in 1947 was crossed by five rivers.
4 H.H. Crosby, *A Wing and a Prayer* (London, Robson, 1993).
5 The Grant of Administration of Maharani Jind Kaur is under 'Jinda Kower'.
6 Freda Barbara (1997), resident of Old Buckenham.
7 Old Buckenham and Blo Norton visitors' book (1897 to 1926), Private Collection.
8 *Morning Post*, 9 October 1926.

Bibliography

Aijazuddin, F.S., *Sikh Portraits By European Artists*, London, Sotheby Parke Bernet, 1979

Alexander, M., and Anand, S., *Queen Victoria's Maharajah*, London, Weidenfeld & Nicolson, 1980

Atkinson, Diane, *The Suffragettes in Pictures*, Stroud, Sutton Publishing, 1996

Bell, E., *The Annexation of the Punjaub & the Maharajah Duleep Singh*, London, Trubner & Co., 1882

Borch, Jakab, *The Blue Hare; Hare-Hawking in the 19th Century*, London, 1896

Campbell, Christy, *The Maharajah's Box*, London, HarperCollins, 2000

Cunningham, Joseph Davey, *The History of the Sikhs from the Origin of the Nation to the Battles of the Sutlej*, London, John Murray, 1849

Cyon, Elie de., *Histoire de l'Entente Franco-Russe, Mémoires et Souvenirs*, Paris, 1895

Gladstone, Hugh. *Record Bags and Shooting Records*, 2nd edn, London, H.F. Witherby, 1930

Griffin, L.H., *Rulers of India: Ranjit Singh and the Sikh Barrier between our Growing Empire and Central Asia*, London, OUP, 1916

Hall, R., *Lovers on the Nile*, Devon, Readers Union, 1980

Khan, F.A., *The Princess Bamba Collection: Antiquities of Sikh Period*, Lahore, Department of Archaeology, 1961

Lascelles, Rt Hon Gerald, *Thirty-five Years in the Forest*, London, Edward Arnold, 1915

Login, Lady, *Sir John Login & Duleep Singh*, London, W.H. Allen, 1890

Login, E. Dalhousie, *Lady Login's Recollections*, London, John Murray, 1916

Omissi, David, *Indian Voices of the Great War: Soldiers' Letters, 1914–18*, Basingstoke, Macmillan, 1999

Osgood, Julian [Anon], *Uncensored Recollections*, London, Nash & Grayson, 1924

Pearse, Hugh, *Soldier and Traveller: The Memoirs of Alexander Gardner*, Edinburgh & London, William Blackwood, 1898

Shaw, D., *London in the Sixties by One of the Old Brigade*, London, Everett & Co., 1914

Singh, Bhagat, *The Sikh Misals*, Patiala, Punjabi University, 1993

Singh, Duleep, *The Maharajah Duleep Singh & the Government*, London, Trubner & Co., 1884

Singh, Frederick Duleep, *Portraits in Norfolk Portraits*, ed. E. Farrer, Jarrolds, 1928

Singh, Ganda, *Maharajah Duleep Singh Correspondence*, Patiala, Punjabi University, 1977

——, *Private Correspondence relating to the Anglo-Sikh Wars*, Patiala, Sikh History Society, 1955

Smyth, Carmichael, *The Reigning Family of Lahore*, Calcutta, W. Thacker & Co., 1847

Sutherland, Dennis, *'His Highness Prince Frederick Duleep', East Anglian Magazine* (September 1976), pp. 434–7

Suri, S.L., *Umdat-Ut-Twarikh 1885–1889*, Lahore, Arya Press, 1961

Tandon, Prakash, *Punjabi Century*, London, Chatto & Windus, 1961

Turner, T.W., *Memoirs of a Gamekeeper: Elveden, 1868–1953*, London, Geoffrey Bles, 1954

Acknowledgements and Picture Credits

I would firstly like to thank my family, my mother, father and wife Satnam for their continued support and encouragement throughout this long project.

I am very grateful to the following for making this book possible: Mr Adalbert Muller of Switzerland for access to Muller family papers and photographs; Marion Fontious of Munich for introducing me to the whole Muller family; Dr Hendrik Schmidt of Essen, Germany, for his archival material; Mrs Oriel Sutherland; Mrs Catherine Alexdrowna Oxley for her unrivalled collection and personal recollections of her godmother Princess Sophia; Sardar Beant Singh Sandhawalia and his son Sukhdev Singh of Amritsar, Punjab, for their assistance and use of family papers and photographs.

I would like to thank Isis Quaresma-Cabral, Paris, for her invaluable assistance and French knowledge, research and translations; F.S. Aijazuddin of Lahore; Ankar Singh Rathore; Nanaki, Satkartar and Simran Bance; Harminder Singh Bal; Tony Paul; Narinder Singh Dosanjh; Robert Scoales; Ranjit Singh Lohia; Dr Chanan Singh Chan; Paramjit Singh; Mr Harbinder Singh Rana of the Maharajah Duleep Singh Centenary Trust; T. Sher Singh of Canada, and Dr Narinder Kapany and Chintan Singh of the Sikh Foundation USA.

I am personally grateful to the following for their local knowledge, personal recollections and archives: Len Brown, evacuee to Blo Norton, on his local knowledge and background information on the principal characters surrounding the Princesses; Mr Francis Hoare for his valuable time and assistance; Shirley Phimister; Ernest Shaw; Leslie Mutum; Winfred Rae of Hampton House; the late Allan Walker from Perthshire, for information of Duleep Singh's infant son; Stephen Govier; Clive Payne; Christy Campbell; Anthea Du Rose; Bruce Reeves; Lillian Coram; Doris Kettle; Hilda Andrews; the late Mrs Michael Watson; Sid Hammond; John Mayes; Freda Barbara; John Gaze; Ellis Clarke; Myrtle Barret; Mr P.G. Ashpitel, the grandson of Tommy Scott; Neville Turner; Dr Gerda Schaefer and Dr Rudolf Lambert of Kassel, Germany.

A special thank you to the Ancient House Museum for use of their records and collections, especially to the curator Mr Oliver Bone and all the staff for their continued support and assistance over the last few years; George Menzies of Castle Menzies and the Menzies Trust; Thetford library, Sue Holt for access to Prince Frederick's collection and images, and team librarian Jean Archdeacon; Malcolm of Thetford; Whitby Archives & Heritage Centre, Sylvia Hutchinson for all her help and assistance in finding so much information on the Whitby connection; the Suffolk & Norfolk Yeomanry Trust; Neil Storey from the Muckleborough Collection, for his valuable Norfolk Yeomanry knowledge; Monsieur Coppo and Monsieur Pierre of the Somotha Association in Monte Carlo; the Cimetière de Monaco, and Georges Marsan the Mairie de Monaco; Helen Gray for tracking down the images relating to the family and Miss Frances Dimond, curator of the Royal Photograph Collection including all the staff at the Royal Archives, Windsor Castle, material from which is published by gracious permission of Her Majesty Queen Elizabeth II.

I wish to thank the archivists and staff of the Norfolk Records Office; Paddington Library; Westminster Archives; Inverness Museum; National Army Museum; Golders Green Crematorium; Norwich & Norfolk Archaeological Society; Bury Records Office; Suffolk Records Office (Ipswich); The Suffolk & Norfolk Yeomanry Trust; The British Library and the Oriental & India Office collection; Osborne House, Isle of

Wight; *Eastern Daily Press* Picture Library, Norwich; Gloucestershire Records Office; Museum of London, Julie Cochrane, Gail Cameron for the Suffragette material relating to Princess Sophia; The US Military Academy, West Point NY; The Victoria & Albert Museum; Bridgeman Art Library; University of Newcastle, The Robinson Library, Gertrude Bell archive; Department of Archaeology & Museums at Karachi and the Princess Bamba Collection, Lahore Fort; the Hon. Lord Iveagh for also giving me access to Elveden Hall; my editor Jaqueline Mitchell and also Elizabeth Stone and all staff at Sutton Publishing, and a very special thank you to Amandeep Singh Madra for his support, precious time and assistance in making this book possible.

Last but not least, to the Almighty for giving me the strength and guidance to carry out such a project.

The author and publisher are grateful to the following for permission to reproduce copyright material. Pages Nos, t=top, b=bottom. Ancient House Museum: 41t, 48, 53b, 55t, 57b, 63t, 79, 91b, 97t, 100, 105, 108b, 116b, 130, 131t, 139t; The Royal Collection 2004, Her Majesty Queen Elizabeth II: 30b, 31t, 32b, 42, 107t, 116t; Mr Adalbert Muller: 45, 63b, 107b; Dr Hendrik Schimdt: 40, 41b, 52, 109; Mrs Catherine Alexadrowna Oxley: 90b, 99t, 101t, 111b, 112t, 118t, 121b, 122t, 122b, 123t, 126, 132b, 134t; Sardar Beant Singh Sandhawalia: 64b, 119t, 119b, 134b; Thetford Library: 49, 50t, 50b, 57t, 58, 59t, 60t, 72b, 89b, 102t; The Suffolk & Norfolk Yeomanry Trust: 92, 93b, 94,97b; Dr Narinder Singh Kapany Sikh Foundation USA: 37t; Gloucester Records Office: 37b; National Army Museum: 24t; Whitby Archives & Heritage Centre: 33b; The British Library: 69t, 69b; EDPpics2004: 103b, 104b; Museum of London: 120, 121t; US Military Academy, West Point, NY (1901) 32nd Annual Reunion of the Association of the Graduates of the USMA: 70t; The Victoria & Albert Museum Lafayette L2251: 117t; Bridgeman Art Library: 60b; Menzies Charitable Trust: 33t; Dr Chana Singh Chan: 133t; Tony Paul: 91t; Paramjit Singh: 23t, 38b, 61; Narinder Singh Dosanjh: 139b; Shirley Phimster: 124, 125t, 125b; Malcolm of Thetford: 53t, 53t; Olive Shickle: 131b; Allan Walker (late): 44t, 141b; Rachel Wilson: 95b, 96t, 96b; Gerry Moore: 117b; Brian Setchell: 146b; Kathleen Wade: 110b. 112b; Myrtle Barrett: 98, 101b; P.G. Ashpitel: 26b; Dr Rudolf Lambert: 111t; Sid Hammond: 68; Ankar Singh Rathore: 6; Len Brown: 144b, 145b; Bob Scoales: 23b; Private Collections: 19, 39t, 77t, 81b, 83, 84b, 90t, 95t, 99b, 147t; Lahore Fort Museum Princess Bamba Collection: 21; Maharajah Duleep Singh Centenary Trust: 146t. All other images are from the author's personal collection.

Index

Page number in italics refer to illustrations

Ada Duleep Singh, Maharani 67–8, 70, 71, 73, 74, 81, 136, 146
 wedding 73
Ahmed Shah Abdali 11
Albert Edward Duleep Singh, Prince 73, 74, 79, *80*, 106, 108, 114, *116*
 birth 51, 76
Albert, Edward, Prince of Wales 16, 31–2, *38*, 46–7, *54–5*, 61, 70, 74
 wife of *60*, 61
Albert, Prince Consort 10, 29, 52, 77
Alexander III, Tsar 71, 73
Alfred, Prince, Duke of Saxe-Gotha 10, 31, 38, *61*
Amritsar 12, 18, 106, 122, 133, 147
Anne Duleep Singh, Princess (Lady Anne Blanche Coventry) 76, *82–4*, *104*, *116*, *136*, *137*, 142, 145, 146
Aroor Singh *53*, *60*, 61, 74
Arthur, Prince, Duke of Connaught 10
Ash, Polly (Ashted) 47, 67

Bamba Duleep Singh, Princess (Sutherland) 61, *62–3*, 82, 104, 112, *113*, 114, 145–7
 birth 51, *127*, 128
 childhood *108*, *109*, *130–1*
 and India 122, 129, *132–3*
 latter years *133*, *134*
 death of *134*, 136, 147
Bamba, Maharani (Muller) *40*, 41–2, *43*, 51, *56–8*, 60, *62*, *70*, 76, 107
 firstborn *44*, 141
 death of *72*, 73, 81
Bell, Gertrude 84
Blo Norton 104, 124, 125, 128, 131, 133, 138, 145, *146*
 Hall 86, *99*, *102*, 114, 122, *144*
 Temple *99*
Budh Singh 11, 12

Cambridge, Duke of *55*
Casey, Patrick 69, 70, 71
Catherine Duleep Singh, Princess 61, *62*, *90*, 104, 123, *116*, 120, 124, 136, 145, 146
 birth 51, 106
 childhood *79*, *105*, *107*, *108*, *109*, *130*
 relations with Lina 110–11
 death of 112, 128
Charhat Singh 11
Chattar Singh Attariwala 15, 28
Cyon, Elie de *69*, 70

Dalhousie, Lord 15, 19, 20, 25, 28, 29–30, *38*, 39, 62, 63, 145
Duleep Singh, Maharajah 6, 16, *21*, *24*, 26, *27*, *29*, *30*, *32*, 38, 44, 61, 62, *63*, *65*, 80, 90, 119, 123, 138–41, 145
 ancestry 11
 coming to the throne 13, 14, *17*
 birth 18
 conversion to Christianity 20, 25, 30
 submission *22*, *24*, 15, 25
 marriage 28, 34, *42*, 40
 in England 33, *34–5*
 Europe 40, *45*, *68*, 69, *70*, 71, 73
 India 36, *40*, 76, 23
 extravagant life 46–7, *52*, *54–5*, *57*, 59, *60*
 re-conversion to Sikhism 66–7
 arrest 66–7
 death 74, 136

East India Company 18, 24, 29, 34
Elveden 54, 67, 79, 89, 102, 136
 Hall *16*, 37, 44, 46, *48–50*, *53*, *56–7*, *135*, *140*
 church *50*, *72*, *139*

Fatehgarh 19, 20, 26, 62
Frederick Duleep Singh, Prince *52*, *56*, 61, *62*, 70, 73, 74, 82, *90–1*, *97*, 129, 131, 138, 143–4, 146–6
 birth 51, 76, 86
 childhood *85*, *88–9*
 interest 86–7
 sporting 53, *58*, 78, *84*, *100*, *102*, 143
 military service *92–7*
 latter years *98–100*
 museum *103*
 death *104*, *122*, *145*

Gouramma, Victoria *34*, 43

Hardinge, Henry 14, *22*, 23, 62
Hatherop, Castle *37*, 141, 142
Hookum Singh 52, *53*, *60*, 62

Irene Duleep Singh, Princess 73, *146*
Iveagh, Lord 51, *100*, *102*, 140

Jawahar Singh 18
Jind 106
  Raja of, 11
Jind Kaur, Maharani 14, 18, *23*, 36, *37*, 82, 114, 142
  birth 13
  death 39, 41, 132

Katkov, Mikhail *69*, *70*, 71, 73
Kharak Singh 12, 13
Koh-i-noor 10, 30, 25

Lahore 10, 12, 13, 15, *16*, 18, 25, 29, 48, 122, 128, 129, 133, 147
  Fort 14, 21
Lawrence, Henry 14, 28
Leopold, Prince 10, 31
Login, John 15, 18, 20, 21, 29, *25*, *28*, 32, 36, 38, 39, 62, 142
  death 39
Login, Lena *26*, 28, 32, 33, 41, 43, 66, 90

Manna Singh Aulakh 13, 14
Mehtab Kaur 11
Mahan Singh, 6, 11–12, 106
  tomb of, *6*
Menzies, Robert 33
  Castle *33*, 141
Misals 11–12
Mulgrave Castle *33*, 37, 46, 141
Muller, Charlotte Maria *108*
Muller, Karl Wilhelm *107*, 128
Muller, Thomas Ludwig *41*, 42, 129
Muller, Wilhelm Alexander *107*

Naudh Singh 11
Naunihal Singh, Prince 12, 13

Oliphant, Arthur 79
Oliphant, James 33, 41, 56, 58, 66
Osgood, Julian 46, 67–8

Pauline Duleep Singh, Princess 73, 104, 136, 145, 146
Pratap Singh, Prince 13
Punjab 6, 11–13, 16, 19, 41, 62–3, 68, 74, 104, 128–9, 133–4, 138
  British enter 14
  annexation 15

Ranjit Singh, Maharajah, 9, 13, 14, 16, 18, *19*, 25, 64, 101, 106, 115, 132, 134
  birth 12
  tomb of *132*

Sada Kaur 11,12
Sandhawalia 13
  Ajit Singh *22*
  Thakur Singh *64*, 73, 119
  Pritam Singh *119*, 122, 128, 134
  Gurdit Singh *64*, 119
  Beant Singh *134*, *147*
  Sukhdev Singh *147*
Schoefft, August 21, 48, 101
Schafer, Fraulein 'Lina' 106, *110*, 111, 128, 138
Scott, Thomas *26*
Sher Singh, Maharajah 13, 18, 21, 101
  wife of 20, 28
  death *22*
Sheikhapura, *23*
Sikh Wars 15–15, 17, 19, 22–3, 63
Sophia, Duleep Singh 61, *62*, 82, *84*, *90*, 104, *121*, 136, 138, 145, 146
  birth 51, *113*, 114
  childhood 79, *108*, *109*, 116
  suffragette 114–15, *120–1*, *123*
  spinster years *112*, *117*, *118*, *122*
  links with India *115*, *119*, *122*, *123*, 132
  and war evacuees *124–5*
  death *126*
Sukarchakkia (Misal) 11–12
Sutherland, Col David Waters 122, 128

Tevis, General Charles Carroll *70*, 71, 73
Torry, Lt J.S.A. 147

Victor Duleep Singh, Prince 10, 52, 56, 61, *62*, 70, 74, 80, 88, 91, 116, 146
  birth *51*, 76, 77
  and sport 53, 58, *75*, *78*, *81*, *84*
  marriage 82
  death 84, 136–7, 142
Victoria, Queen 10, 29–31, 33, 47–8, 50–1, 52, *62*, 69, 73, 74, 76, 77, 82, 93, 118, 143
Villament, Pierre Marie 146

Wetheril, Ada *see* Ada Duleep Singh, Maharani
Winterhalter, Franz Xaver 30, 48, 140